D0617376

Ben Jonson's Poesis
A Literary Dialectic of Ideal and History

Jongsook Lee

Ben Jonson's Poesis

A Literary Dialectic of Ideal and History

University Press of Virginia   *Charlottesville*

THE UNIVERSITY PRESS OF VIRGINIA
Copyright © 1989 by the Rector and Visitors
of the University of Virginia

First published 1989

LIBRARY OF CONGRESS
Library of Congress Cataloging-in-Publication Data

Lee, Jongsook, 1952–
    Ben Jonson's poesis : a literary dialectic of ideal and history /
Jongsook Lee.
        p. cm.
    Revision of thesis (Ph. D.)
    Bibliography: p.
    ISBN 0-8139-1192-3
    1. Jonson, Ben, 1573?–1637—Criticism and interpretation.
2. Historical poetry, English—History and criticism. 3. Historical
drama, English—History and criticism. 4. Laudatory poetry.
English—History and criticism. 5. Mimesis in literature.
I. Title.
PR2642.H5L44 1989
822'.3—dc19   88-17262
                                                    CIP

Printed in the United States of America

To Thomas Clayton

Contents

Acknowledgments

Although he disclaims it, I owe the greatest debt of gratitude to Thomas Clayton, the supervisor of the dissertation from which this book emerged. He has helped so much to bring this book into the world that I cannot claim it as my own without doing him less than justice.

I owe important debts to many friends and colleagues. I am grateful to Janis Lull, Constance Braden, Wilma Evans, Scott Pitman, and Paul Munn for their friendship and encouragement. David Haley and Stanford E. Lehmberg at the University of Minnesota and Hee-Jin Park and Nak-Chung Paik at Seoul National University read the typescript at the earlier stages of its preparation and gave helpful comments. Thanks are due to the staff of the University Press of Virginia, especially its late director, Walker Cowen, for his kindness, and the two anonymous readers for their valuable suggestions which have made revision rewarding in itself. Whatever shortcomings remain are, of course, no one's responsibility but my own.

In somewhat different form, chapter 1 was published in the January 1986 issue of *Journal of English and Germanic Philology,* © 1986 by the Board of Trustees of the University of Illinois. I am grateful to *JEGP* and to its publisher, the University of Illinois Press, for permission to reprint.

My husband Jong-Chun Cha and my son Seung know how much I owe to them and how much I shall continue to owe.

A Note on Texts

The standard text of Jonson's works remains *Ben Jonson,* ed. C. H. Herford and Percy and Evelyn Simpson, 11 vols. (Oxford: Clarendon, 1925–52). All references to Jonson's works are made to this edition and are incorporated in the text. Works and collections of Jonson that I have cited frequently in the text by title, and the volume and pages that contain them, are as follows:

Epigrammes 8:21–90
Forest 8:91–122
Underwood 8:123–296
Ungathered Verse 8:357–423
Catiline 5:409–550
Sejanus 4:327–471
Cynthia's Revels 4:1–184
Love Restored 7:373–85
Mercury Vindicated from the Alchemists at Court 7:407–17

Quotations from these are identified by line numbers in the text rather than given in redundant footnotes. Citations of other works of Jonson are identified by the title, the abbreviation *H&S* and volume number, and page and line numbers. The spelling of titles has been modernized, and i/j and u/v spelling forms have been regularized.

All quotations from Sidney's *Defence of Poetry* are from *Miscellaneous Prose of Sir Philip Sidney,* ed. Katherine Duncan-Jones and Jan Van Dorsten (Oxford: Clarendon, 1973).

Ben Jonson's Poesis
A Literary Dialectic of Ideal and History

Introduction

The problem of how to reconcile fact and fiction is not peculiar to Jonson. It confronts every writer who tries to include statements about an ideal world in a representation of the world of particular facts. But the problem remained Jonson's major concern throughout his career and frequently became the subject of his poetry itself. This study examines the history of the conflict between fact and fiction in Jonson—its roots and its consequences in the nature and tone of his work.

The most obvious expression of Jonson's allegiance to the world of particular facts is his realistic satire, a form in which he displays his intimate knowledge of "every corner and alley of crowded, reeking, picturesque London" (*H&S* 1:121). But what drives him to an imitation of the factual world is his impulse to reform that world in conformity with his ideals. His impatience with the world as it is, is recognizable even in the unflattering portraits we read of him: for the obviously intimidated William Drummond of Hawthornden, Jonson was "a great lover and praiser of himself, a contemner and Scorner of others" (*Conversations H&S* 1:151.680–81); for Edmund Wilson, he was an "anal erotic," pedantic, arrogant, irritable, and stubborn; for Arthur Marotti, he "is an artistic schizophrenic, with both a Dionysian and an Apollonian side"; for Ian Donaldson, he is a man whose anger with human follies characterizes everything he wrote; and more recently, for John Gordon Sweeney, he shows "ambivalence to authority and the confusion of self-interest with social service and aggression with instruction."[1] His realism—his unrelenting eye for the facts of the world—takes root in his idealism and enters the service of the actualization of ideals: by representing the exact image of the world as it is, he tries to indicate the necessity, and the possibility, of remaking the world into something better. The relationship between Jonson's realism and idealism can better be described in his own words:

> Not to know vice at all, and keepe true state,
> Is vertue, and not *Fate*:
> Next, to that vertue, is to know vice well,
> And her blacke spight expell.
>
> (*Forest* 11, "Epode," 1–4)

But the main *locus* of interactions between the two impulses is Jonson's celebratory poetry—his poems of praise and court masques. It is true that the impulse to idealize the world is in perilous contiguity to the satiric impulse: praising the world for what it should be but is not is a form of dispraise. But in Jonson's celebratory poetry, expressions of the two impulses are literally juxtaposed. Epigrams of blame are put side by side with epigrams of praise, and the masque includes not only the idealistic vision of the main masque but also the realistic world of the antimasque. Realistic pictures of the factual world, when presented with its idealized images, inevitably change the reader's response to those idealized images: they become commentaries on the idealization itself.

Jonson's dual allegiance to fact and fiction is in part a response to the contradictions inherent in Renaissance theories of poetry. The Renaissance attitude toward literary mimesis was determined by the necessity to defend poetry from the Platonic charge that mimesis is a pernicious lie, a charge revived in England with renewed vehemence by Puritan "poet-haters" like Stephen Gosson. As O. B. Hardison, Bernard Weinberg, Baxter Hathaway, and Brian Vickers have noted, Renaissance defenders of poetry had to answer the Puritan detractors of the art on their own ground—the moral value of poetry.[2] Sidney, availing himself of the Aristotelian idea of mimesis as an imitation of universal nature, countered the attack with the claim that poetic mimesis is fiction, but a fiction truer than fact and of greater moral value. Poetry edifies and reforms the world by imitating idealized images of human nature. It moves the reader to virtuous action, because it represents not the "foolish world" with all its contradictions, but a "golden world," in which virtue always prevails over vice. In short, Sidney's claim rests in the main on poetry's epideictic function: like epideictic oratory, it praises the virtuous and blames the vicious.

But as Vickers observes, the Sidneian double emphasis on poetry's fictionality and its epideictic power presented the Renaissance with another dilemma between fact and fiction. Epideictic oratory, at least in theory, is about actual persons and actual events. It describes the fortune, nature, and character of a historical person. Moreover, its persuasive power depends in large part on its truth as a representation of fact. By compounding poetry with epideictic oratory, the Renaissance was faced with the problem of how to reconcile history and poetry, factual matter and fictional form.

The tension between fact and fiction was made more acute by the sharp distinction between history and poetry made by Sidney, who himself was influenced by the emerging historicism and its emphasis on the verifiable as the proper domain of history. Sidney distinguished history from poetry, saying that history reported the particular and the factual while poetry imitated the universal and the ideal. The distinction denied poetry the status of historical fact, which it had enjoyed from antiquity. This definition of poetry as fictive inevitably clashed with the Renaissance, and Sidney's own, identification of poetry and epideictic oratory, assigning poetry to the space between history and poetry, description and idealization. And as Brian Vickers puts it, "how to reconcile the supposedly factual content of epideictic with its poetic or fictive mode was a problem not all Renaissance theorists solved."[3]

As a praiser of the king and his courtiers, as an epideictic poet with a strong bias toward realism, Jonson is faced with the necessity of resolving the tension between fact and fiction not merely in theory but in his writing. One of the most revealing courses he takes to solve the problem is to direct the reader's attention to the problem itself by commenting on and theorizing about the process of turning fact into fiction. His work abounds in meta-commentaries: his poems of praise are often commentaries on the act of praising; his plays invariably include plays-within-the-play, or plays-within-the-play-within-the-play; and his later court masques concern masques and masquing occasions. Not only the sheer abundance of these meta-commentaries on the mimetic process but also their effect upon the reader is suggestive: they disrupt the illusion of factuality that his mimesis aims at creating; by exposing the artificiality of his mimesis, and by diverting the reader's attention from the mimesis to the mimetic process itself, they interfere with the reader's experience of his mimesis; and, finally, by making it clear that his mimesis is a fiction and not a fact, they reinforce the status of the mimesis as a fact. By means of these meta-commentaries, then, Jonson prevents the reader's uncritical immersion in the fictional world of his mimesis and, at the same time, attempts to achieve a greater fidelity to the factual world. In effect, he expands the limit of literary mimesis to include another kind of mimesis—a mimesis of the mimetic process itself.

The first two chapters of this book are case studies of Jonson's methods of translating facts into statements about ideal persons and the society they create, using works that have been regarded either as true representations of an actual person (the two contrasting poems on Cecilia Bulstrode: *Under-*

wood 49 and *Ungathered Verse* 9) or as literal dramatizations of what have been received as historical facts (the two Roman tragedies, *Sejanus* and *Catiline*). The process of turning actual persons or historical *données* into highly idealized images of human nature generates some tension between fact and fiction, the source of the anxiety that makes Jonson insist on the factual truth of his idealized pictures. How this tension manifests itself in the text of a poem, and how Jonson resolves it, are the subjects of the next two chapters, "Fact and Fiction in Jonson's Epideictic Poetry" and "Jonson's Meta-Masques and the Poet King." The tension between fact and fiction can best be seen in the meta-commentaries, which abound in Jonson's poems of praise and court masques, and which increasingly become his major solution to the problem of reconciling fact and fiction.

Viewed from a larger perspective of Jonson's commitment to the Renaissance Humanist program of reforming the world, the conflict between fact and fiction in his poetry finally becomes a problem of how to control the audience. The Humanist poetic scheme, which conceives of the "ending end" of poetry as moving the reader to virtuous action, depends for its success on the reader—his correct understanding of what the poet has to say. Should the reader misinterpret the poet's intention, the whole didactic scheme would fail. Jonson's problem as an epideictic poet, then, includes how to minimize the danger of misinterpretation, how to reduce the reader's fictionalizing, and how to counter effectively the fictions the reader brings to the text, those fictions which he maintains about the world and himself.

The concluding chapter, " 'Rare Poems Aske Rare Friends': The Poet and the Reader in *Epigrammes*," analyzes Jonson's authorial assertiveness—his constant theorizing about the relationship between art and society, and the specific methods he uses to secure maximum communication with the reader—concentrating on his *Epigrammes* and his numerous prefaces, addresses to the reader, dedicatory epistles, and prologues and epilogues. Jonson's effort to create a greater factuality for his poetic fiction is a part of his strategy to control the audience's response to his poetry, to prevent them from confusing fact and fiction, bringing them, through truth, to such perfectibility as the world with all its limitations nevertheless permits and a better human condition positively demands.

1

Biography into Poetry

Cecilia Bulstrode and Jonson's Epideictics

A. C. Swinburne found in Jonson's "Epigram on the Court Pucell" (*Underwood* 49) something of an eruption of misogyny, which he thought represented Jonson's attitude toward women in general, despite his ardent idealization of womanhood in the tributes to his patronesses:

The "epigram" or rather satire "on the Court Pucelle" goes beyond even the licence assumed by Pope in the virulent ferocity of its personal attack on a woman. This may be explained, or at least illustrated, by the fact that Ben Jonson's views regarding womanhood in general were radically cynical though externally chivalrous: a charge which can be brought against no other poet or dramatist of his age. He could pay more splendid compliments than any of them to this or that particular woman . . . but no man has said coarser (I had well-nigh written, viler) things against the sex to which these exceptionally honored patronesses belonged.[1]

Half a century later, Jonson's Oxford editors, C. H. Herford and Percy and Evelyn Simpson, found the epigram a tastelessly coarse personal attack on Cecilia Bulstrode and repeated Swinburne's charge:

The marked and painted Court beauty attracted with peculiar readiness the cynical regard, which for him—a few chosen women friends set apart—habitually disrobed womankind of even ordinary grace and virtue. . . . For the most part the welter of personal antagonism, quarrel, and intrigue which lies behind these diatribes escapes our scrutiny. But in one case at least the woman at whom he levels his scorn in these years can be identified. What Jonson's special quarrel with Cecily Bulstrode was, we do not know. Certainly few men in his day, or in any day, have assailed a woman with the foul-mouthed ferocity of his lines to "The Court Purcell" (*Underwoods,* xlix). . . . But Jonson impatiently flings aside the dignity of just rebuke (which indeed he had little title to administer), in order to outdo her in ribald abuse. (*H&S* 1:58–59)

In these responses to the epigram, one might detect a touch of romantic prejudice against satire, or even of Victorian prudery. But these verdicts seem to stem in any case from the assumption that Jonson's occasional poems reflect directly the particular events in his experience out of which they arose. Both Swinburne and Jonson's Oxford editors find in the epigram a disturbingly "personal" attack on a woman, which in turn reveals Jonson's "personal" cynicism toward women in general. To agree with them and to read the epigram only as a historical document of Jonson's response to Cecilia Bulstrode is to deny the epigram its place among Jonson's epigrams and other poems, and ultimately its claim as a poem with a context more social and less personal than that merely of the accused and the accuser.[2]

Jonson certainly was not fettered by the facts about Cecilia Bulstrode, his supposed personal feelings against her, or any hidden mysogyny, when he later wrote an epitaph on her death. His "Epitaph on Cecilia Bulstrode" (*Ungathered Verse* 9) in effect retracts the charges he made against her in the epigram point by point, turning the "Court Purcell" into Cynthia, the would-be wit into the tutor to Pallas, the blasphemous idolater into a votary. By dying, Cecilia Bulstrode would seem to have undergone a marvelous sea change in Jonson's mind. What is the secret of this transmutation?

In his commentary on the epitaph, Percy Simpson suggests that Jonson's covering note "To my right worthy Freind M[r]. Geo: Gerrard" sent with the epitaph contains some of the secret.[3] He especially dwells on the lines in the note stating Jonson's response to the news of Cecilia Bulstrode's death: "till your Letter came, I was not so much as acquainted with the sad argument, w[ch] both strooke me and keepes me a heavy man, Would God, I had seene her before that some y[t] live might have corrected some prejudices they had injuriously of mee" (*H&S* 8:372). Simpson questions the sincerity of the statement, which expresses not so much Jonson's genuine feelings for the dead Cecilia Bulstrode as his concerns about "some y[t] live" and their prejudices against him. He suggests that Jonson might have written the eulogistic epitaph to please the "some y[t] live," including perhaps Lucy, Countess of Bedford, his powerful patroness and the cousin and intimate friend of Cecilia Bulstrode, whom he must have offended with his epigram on the "Court Pucell." Anecdotes about the epigram support this view. Jonson read to William Drummond of Hawthornden the "Verses on the Pucelle of the Court Mistriss Boulstred, whose Epitaph Done made" and remarked that the poem "was stollen out of his pocket by a Gentleman who drank him drouisie &

given Mistress Boulstraid, which brought him great displeasur" (*Conversations, H&S* 1:135.103–04, 150.646–48). But Simpson could find still other causes for Jonson's sudden change of attitude toward Cecilia Bulstrode: "Did he, on hearing of his victim's lingering agony, yield to a natural impulse of pity, and writing under pressure, force the note? Or was he honestly convinced that he had slandered her? 'The greater Witts,' who had already penned their eulogies, certainly included Donne, and Donne was a friend whose judgment would weigh powerfully with Jonson. Without Gerrard's letter, we shall have no final solution of the problem" (*H&S* 11:131).

All these conjectures about the relationship between the epigram and the epitaph—written by one and the same poet on one and the same Cecilia Bulstrode—result from a reading of the poems as historical documents of Cecilia Bulstrode's life and Jonson's response to it. Of course, one cannot ignore the historical dimension of poems, especially when they derive part of their identities from their insistence upon it, as Jonson's poems on historical persons do.[4] But Jonson himself more than once indicates that his poems are not always faithful to facts: in Epigram 65, "To My Muse," he recognizes his poetry's dangerous power to transform fact into fiction, a "worthlesse lord" into a "great image." He also wishes to be judged more by his skill in shaping poetic fictions than by his fidelity to historical facts: dedicating the *Epigrammes* to William, Earl of Pembroke, he says "if I have praysed, unfortunately, any one, that doth not deserve; or, if all answer not, in all numbers, the pictures I have made them: I hope it will be forgiven me, that they are no ill pieces, though they be not like the persons" (*H&S* 8:26.21–25).

Even if Jonson were faithful to facts in his two contradictory pictures of Cecilia Bulstrode, we have no way of testing their truth. Indeed, the paucity of historical facts about Cecilia Bulstrode available to us makes it impossible even to tell which of the two pictures represents the real Cecilia Bulstrode. We know very little about her, much less her association with Jonson.[5] She was the daughter of Edward Bulstrode, of Hadgerley Bulstrode, Buckinghamshire, was baptized at Beaconsfield on February 12, 1583/4, and died at the Earl of Bedford's house at Twickenham on August 4, 1609. How she spent her "short day of frost and sun" (in Walter Pater's phrase), we do not know, except that as her brother-in-law, Sir James Whitelocke, tells us in his *Liber Familicus,* she was a gentlewoman of the bedchamber to Queen Anne.[6] Of her dying days we have a better record. In his letter to Sir Henry Goodyer, Donne describes her last illness thus:

I fear earnestly that Mistresse *Bolstrod* will not escape that sicknesse in which she labours at this time. I sent this morning to ask of her passage of this night; and the return is, that she is as I left her yesternight, and then by the strength of her understanding, and voyce, (proportionally to her fashion, which was ever remisse) by the eavennesse and life of her pulse, and by her temper, I could allow her long life, and impute all her sicknesse to her minde. But the History of her sicknesse, makes me justly fear, that she will scarce last so long, as that you when you receive this letter, may do her any good office, in praying for her; for she hath not for many days received so much as a preserved Barbery, but it returns, and all accompanied with a Fever, the mother, and an extream ill spleen. (*Letters,* 215–16)

And then the short, impersonal note in the Twickenham Registers informs us that "M^ris Boulstred out of the parke, was buried ye 6th of August 1609." And a year later, a quack, Francis Anthony, in his "Medicinae Chymicae, et veri potabilis Auri assertio" (1610), claimed that after six of the College of Medicine had failed, he had cured "virgo Caecilia Boulstred, aetatis circiter viginti annorum."

Of the cause of her mental anguish, the "extream ill spleen," we know nothing. For the rest of her story we have to turn to a handful of poems on her, in which she chiefly lives. The portraits of Cecilia Bulstrode by various hands make a Marvellean "Gallery": the "Wench at Court" in "An Elegie" ("True Love findes witt") by Jonson's intimate friend Sir John Roe; the supplier of "one poore houres love" for a cynical libertine in "An Elegie to M^ris Boulstred: 1602" ("Shall I goe force an Elegie?") by the same Roe; the "Court Pucell" in Jonson's epigram; a helpless prey of the ravenous Death in Donne's "Elegie on M^ris Boulstred" ("Death I recant"); the "christall" body with a soul of "Paradise" and a heart burning with "sacred fire" in Donne's "Elegie upon the Death of Mistress Boulstred" ("Language thou art too narrow"); the "clearer soul" called to "endless rest" in Lucy, Countess of Bedford's "Elegy" ("Death be not proud"); a paragon of virtue in Jonson's "Epitaph"; and the "noble soul" transcending "the low pitch of earthly things" in Edward, Lord Herbert of Cherbury's "Epitaph. Caecil. Boulstr. quae post languescentem morbum non sine inquietudine spiritus & conscientiae obiit."[7] The dissimilarities between the portraits of Cecilia Bulstrode alive and dead defy attempts to restore even a coherent general character of her life.

But the problem of disparity between the two Jonson portraits might not exist if we were not concerned *mainly* with the historical truth about the relationship between Jonson and Cecilia Bulstrode, which may or may not have made its way into the poems. What is important for the appreciation of the poems as works of art, related to and functioning within larger social and historical contexts than those of their immediate occasions, is to recognize and attempt to define the conventions by means of which Jonson could adopt Cecilia Bulstrode as a member of the community his poetry creates. Indeed, Jonson's contradictory treatments of Cecilia Bulstrode throw an illuminating light on his epideictics, the process through which he transforms a pucelle into a Cynthia, or a Cynthia into a pucelle.

It is true that there are several points specific enough to invite reading the poems as historical documents: the accusation made in the first line of the epigram has a personal note in it. There seems to be the rage and scorn of a spurned man burning with a desire for revenge: "Do's the Court-Pucell then so censure me, / And thinkes I dare not her?" (1–2). The specification of the number of perjuries the court pucelle committed is another example: "And trust her I would least, that hath forswore / In Contract twice, what can shee perjure more?" (29–30). And the details about her fits of hysteria fit well into Donne's account of her last illness, and the quack's claim to have cured it:

> The wits will leave you, if they once perceive
>   You cling to Lords, and Lords, if them you leave
> For Sermoneers: of which now one, now other,
>   They say you weekly invite with fits o'th'Mother,
> And practise for a Miracle.   (37–41)

The epitaph contains still fewer specific allusions to Cecilia Bulstrode's life than the epigram. But the first of her many virtues—that of being a virgin in the Court—seems an unusual one to be praised:

> It covers, first, a Virgin; and, then, one
> That durst be that in Court; a Vertu' alone
> To fill an Epitaph.   (3–5)

The allusion to Chaucer's *Legend of Good Women* in the last line of the epitaph might be saying more than meets the eye. The women Chaucer represents as "good" are Cleopatra, Dido, Hypsipyle, Medea, Lucrece, Ariadne, Philomene, Phyllis, and Hypermnestra. All are presented as being betrayed in love and consequently meeting with tragic deaths. Chaucer uses their stories as exempla against falsehood in love. Cecilia Bulstrode was certainly not in a happy mental state in her dying days. Is the reference to Chaucer's fable meant to be an allusion to the cause of her extreme anguish?

These are the details that might provoke one's curiosity about Cecilia Bulstrode's known and unknown stories. But they are not enough to restrict the poems' contexts to their immediate occasions. In the poems, Jonson is concerned with something more universal and less particular than the things that have happened to Cecilia Bulstrode, and he addresses far more general audiences than Cecilia Bulstrode and those associated with her. In the last half line of the first couplet of the epigram, he directs our attention away from the personal injury and toward the art of censure: "Do's the Court-Pucell then so censure me, / And thinkes I dare not her? *let the world see*" (emphasis mine). Jonson is saying that the epigram will be a showpiece for the world to see how well he could repay her censure with censure. This invitation of the "world" to the arena of verbal parley is similar, in its distancing effect, to his favorite formula for the initiation of the reader into the world of an epitaph: "Reader, stay." The gesture of conscious performance before the eyes of the world in this half line demands a reading of the poems within the context of Jonson's other poems.

In his "Epitaph on Cecilia Bulstrode," Jonson praises the lady for virtues exactly opposite to the vices he has blamed her for in "An Epigram on the Court Pucell." In this turning vices into virtues, Jonson seems to be following what Aristotle teaches about the art of praise and blame in his *Rhetoric.* After prescribing how to praise and blame, Aristotle summarily tells us how one can use the same materials for both purposes: "Thus we have the materials from which encomiums are made, and the materials for reproaches as well. Having our materials on the one side, we at once see those on the other; for blame is derived from the premises directly opposite to those of praise."[8] But Jonson is not so much following Aristotle's precept as being faithful to his perception that praise and blame both appeal to the same value system, the same norm. If poetry of blame is the negative expression of the norm, poetry of praise is its positive one.

One can see the relationship between poems of praise and of blame in Jonson's poetic world most clearly in the *Epigrammes,* the "ripest" of Jonson's studies of humanity. The volume consists of two kinds of epigrams, the commendatory and the satiric. The complementary nature of the relationship between these two kinds of epigrams can best be represented by Jonson's own words. In an epigram of blame, he explains why he studies vices:

> Do what you come for, Captayne, with your news;
>   That's, sit, and eate: doe not my eares abuse.
> I oft looke on False coyne, to know't from true:
>   Not that I love it, more, then I will you.
>   (*Epigrammes* 107, "To Captayne Hungry," 1–4)

To define the true, one must study the false as well; one must have the "exact knowledge of all vertues, and their Contraries" to be able to "render the one lov'd, and the other hated" (*Discoveries, H&S* 8:595). The foolish and the vicious in the satiric epigrams have their antitypes in the virtuous and the rational in the commendatory epigrams; that is, the epigrams of praise provide a normative system, against which the social-moral aberrations portrayed in the epigrams of blame are to be judged. And this is also reflected in the physical arrangements of these two kinds of pictures: Jonson juxtaposes portraits of vices and their opposite virtues. The epigram quoted above, for example, is followed by Epigram 108, "To True Souldiers," whose "high names" Captayne Hungry defiles: "Strength of my Country, whilest I bring to view / Such as are misse-call'd Captaynes, and wrong you; / And your high names" (1–4).[9]

Captayne Hungry turns the name of captain into a term of abuse by not being true to that name; he is a "misse-call'd" captain. The distinction made here between name and identity tells us of the moral significance Jonson attaches to name. In his dedicatory epistle to the Earl of Pembroke, Jonson speaks of how he has made use of the names of the people translated into the "Theatre" of *Epigrammes:*

> In thanks whereof, I returne you the honor of leading forth *so many good and great names (as my verses mention on the better part)* to their remembrance with posteritie. Among whom, if I have praysed unfortunately, any one, that doth not deserve; or, if all answere not, in all numbers, *the pictures I have made of them:* I hope it will be forgiven me, that they are no ill pieces, though they be not like the persons. But I foresee a neerer fate to my booke, then this: that *the vices therein will be own'd before the virtues (though, there, I have avoyded all particulars, as I have done names)* and that some will be so readie to discredit me, as they will have impudence to belye themselves. *(H&S* 8:25–26.17–30; emphasis mine)

Retaining and withholding names is for Jonson an Adam-like activity of giving right names to right persons.[10] By calling them by their true names, he turns them into "pictures" of vices and virtues. Jonson's Epigram 102, "To William Earle of Pembroke," provides a good example of Jonson's use of names in making positive pictures:

> I doe but name thee PEMBROKE, and I find
> It is an *Epigramme,* on all man-kind;
> Against the bad, but of, and to the good.   (1–3)

Pembroke, simply by being himself, becomes a commentary on the world, and his name by itself a tribute more eloquent than any other praise. On the other hand, the vicious are nameless, with only such labels as identify their moral qualities best, as if their actual names were usurped by their overwhelming vices. By losing their names, they lose their humanity and are reduced to specimens of vices, forever pinned down in Jonson's collection as Captayne Hungry, My Lord Ignorant, Sir Cod, Don Surly, A Court-Worm, or A Something, that Walks Somewhere.

Jonson's strategy of idealizing vices and virtues through names leaves its distinctive mark both on the epigram and on the epitaph.[11] When Jonson rechristens Cecilia Bulstrode as "Court Pucell," she ceases to be an individual woman, but is transformed into an archetypal court pucelle. Joining "Court" and "Pucell" together is a significant indicator of the extent of Jonson's idealization: "Purcell" alone would be sufficient to make Cecilia Bulstrode a picture of Iniquity. Throughout the *Epigrammes* Jonson uses sexual amorality as a synecdoche for all forms of moral-social deviation, using "bawd" as a master metaphor for all sorts of moral-social delinquents, from usurers to bad poets. One example sufficiently illustrates this point; Epigram 57, "On Baudes, and Usurers," defines them thus: "If, as their ends, their fruits were so, the same, / Baudrie, and usurie were one kind of game" (1–2).

Those who sell their moral integrity—which, for Jonson, is what makes humans human—for a heap of "dirt" are the same as those who sell their flesh for vanity.[12] "Court" intensifies what "Pucell" has already said. That Jonson, like so many of his contemporaries, viewed the court with scorn is obvious, as a number of epigrams he wrote on its witlings, poetasters, and beauties testify.[13] The court is a negative "school" of manners, as Mill's progress in Epigram 90, "On Mill My Ladies Woman," amply tells us. Or it is a microcosm of a corrupt society, as "A little Shrub growing by" (*Underwood* 21) suggests:

> A parcell of Court-durt, a heape, and masse
>   Of all vice hurled together, there he was,
> Proud, false, and trecherous, vindictive, all
>   That thought can adde, unthankfull, the lay-stall
> Of putrid flesh alive! of blood, the sinke!
>   And so I leave to stirre him, lest he stinke.   (5–10)

By calling Cecilia Bulstrode a whore in the court, Jonson makes her an epitome of Vanity Fair.

"A heape, and masse / Of all vice hurled together," she certainly is: the court pucelle embodies in her own person all the vices Jonson felt bound to pillory in his *Epigrammes*. The specific charges he brings against her in the first six rhetorical questions, beginning with "what though," can be identified as pride, falsity, treachery, and vindictiveness—that is, all sorts of prostitution for vanity. The prime charge Jonson brings against her in the first three questions in lines 3–14 is her intellectual pretensions, which manifest themselves in her abuse and misuse of language, or the "bawdry" of her language:

> What though her Chamber be the very pit
>   Where fight the prime Cocks of the Game, for wit?
> And that as any are strooke, her breath creates
>   New in their stead, out of the Candidates?
> What though with Tribade lust she force a Muse,
>   And in an Epicoene fury can write newes
> Equall with that, which for the best newes goes,
>   As aerie light, and as like wit as those?
> What though she talke, and cannot once with them,
>   Make State, Religion, Bawdrie, all a theame?
> And as lip-thirstie, in each words expence,
>   Doth labour with the Phrase more then the sense?   (3–14)

The enormity of this charge becomes clearer when we consider Jonson's concern for the state of language as an index to the health of a society: "Wheresoever, manners, and fashions are corrupted, Language is. It imitates the publicke riot. The excesse of Feasts, and apparell, are the notes of a sick State; and the wantonnesse of language, of a sick mind" (*Discoveries, H&S* 8:593). Corrupt language is a symptom of a sick society. And the court pucelle's chamber shows, in little, a "Common-Wealth of Learning" turned quite upside down. Poetry, which should offer "to mankind a certaine rule, and Patterne of living well, and happily; disposing us to all Civil offices of Society," is turned into stuff for a game of "Cocks," serving a court pucelle's pleasure (*Discoveries, H&S* 8:636). The act of divine creation, a model for poetic creativity, is coarsened into her restless replacement of fops around her. Her perverse infatuation with the "Muse" inverts the traditional image of a poet ravished by divine fury. And the product of her "Tribade lust" is "newes," which belongs to the order of rumor Captayne Hungry spreads in a tavern. The summary stricture on the court pucelle's "Common-Wealth of Learning" and her pretensions as a wit comes in the form of a Jonsonian formula for abuse of language, the lack of exact correspondence between word and matter: in lines 13–14 Jonson accuses her for laboring with "the Phrase more then the sense."

The court pucelle's "Idolatry" of appearance is what is to be expected from her emphasis on "Phrase" rather than "sense." After all, in Jonson's world corrupt language is a reflection of corrupt manners. As the juxtaposition of "Religion" and "Bawdrie" in line 12 has already anticipated, she exploits "Holy-dayes" for the worship of her own and others' attires:

> What though she ride two mile on Holy-dayes
> > To Church, as others doe to Feasts and Playes,
> To shew their Tires? to view, and to be view'd?
> > What though she be with Velvet gownes indu'd,
> And spangled Petticotes brought forth to eye,
> > As new rewards of her old secrecie? (15–20)

And, to discerning eyes like Jonson's, nothing speaks more loudly of her true moral identity than the "Velvet gownes" and "spangled Petticotes," the "new rewards of her old secrecie." This is also a stock motif in Jonson's satire, in which he consistently uses foppery of dress as a sure sign of moral degeneration. It reduces man to a creature of tailors, as it does the Frenchified English lord in Epigram 88, "On English Mounsieur":

> Or is it some *french* statue? No: 't doth move,
> > And stoupe, and cringe. O then, it needs must prove
> the new *french*-taylors motion, monthly made,
> > Daily to turne in PAULS, and help the trade. (13–16)

More than that, it turns man into a mere case, or a thing, as in Epigram 97, "On the New Motion":

> See you yond'Motion? Not the old *Fa-ding*,
>   Nor Captayne POD, nor yet the *Eltham-thing;*
> But one more rare, and in the case so new:
>   His cloke with orient velvet quite lin'd through,
> His rosie tyes and garters so ore-blowne,
>   By his each glorious parcell to be knowne!   (1–6)

And it turns the court pucelle into "stuffes and Laces, those my Man can buy" (28), as if she is forced to become what she wears.

Dissembling appearance and treachery are near kin. The court pucelle's foppery of language and dress finds its corollary in her "Candle light" beauty, which serves as a snare to take man into perjured contracts of marriage:

> Farthest I am from the Idolatrie
>   To stuffes and Laces, those my Man can buy.
> And trust her I would least, that hath forswore
>   In Contract twice, what can shee perjure more?
> Indeed, her Dressing some man might delight,
>   Her face there's none can like by Candle light   (27–32)

And with this charge, another item of his stock motifs, Jonson makes the court pucelle somewhat akin to the allegorical figure of Bawd, the false world herself, whom he described in much the same terms in *Forest* 4, "To the World: A farewell for a Gentle-woman, vertuous and noble":

> I know thy forms are studied arts
>   Thy subtle wayes, be narrow straits;
> Thy curtesies but sodaine starts,
>   And what thou call'st thy gifts are baits.
> I know too, though thou strut, and paint,
>   Yet art thou both shrunke up, and old,
> That onely fooles make thee a saint,
>   And all thy good is to be sold.
> I know thou whole art but a shop
>   Of toyes, and trifles, traps, and snares,
> To take the weake, or make them stop:
>   Yet art thou falser then thy wares.   (9–20)

The charges leveled against Cecilia Bulstrode are too stylized to be taken as personal. In this epigram, she becomes a generic court pucelle, and by that means, an image of the false world.

If it were not for Drummond's report that Jonson once read him the "Verses on the Pucelle of the Court Mistriss Boulstred, whose Epitaph Done made," we would have no way of identifying the "Court Pucell" as Cecilia

Bulstrode, and indeed we have none in the epigram, where "she" has no other name than "Court Pucell." If the historical Cecilia Bulstrode does reside in Jonson's poems, she should be in the epitaph, where she has a pronounced identity, " '*Sell Boulstred,*" in line 2. But Cecilia Bulstrode is no more herself in the epitaph than in the epigram. In the epitaph, she is idealized into an embodiment of all virtues. Admittedly, idealization of the dead is something to be expected of funeral poems of any kind. But the brevity and incisiveness required of an epitaph become, in Jonson, an effective strategy of idealization: by making reticence an imperative, they facilitate Jonson's transition from the realm of real life, and personal grief (or the lack of it), to the realm of art, and impersonality.[14]

In "Epitaph on Cecilia Bulstrode," this idealization through brevity and reticence is the strategy that determines Jonson's modification of the three topics of epitaph—lamentation, commendation, and consolation.[15] Like "Epitaph on Elizabeth, L. H." (*Epigrammes* 124), this epitaph begins with a claim of "much in little": "Stay, view this stone: And, if thou beest not such, / Read here a little, that thou mayst know much" (1–2). Unless the very act of writing an epitaph bespeaks grief, the grief of the poet is barely suggested in the negative invitation—"And, if thou beest not such [stone]"—with which Jonson intends to exclude the wrong kind of reader. In talking of one's grief, brevity and restraint can be far more eloquent than copia and expansiveness: the grief is more than one can tell. And with this the poet begins to enumerate the reasons why he should be so sorrowful at her death.

The rest of the poem is a catalogue of such reasons—Cecilia Bulstrode's excelling virtues:

> It covers, first, a Virgin; and then, one
> That durst be that in Court: a vertu'alone
> To fill an Epitaph. But she had more.
> She might have claym'd t'have made the Graces four;
> Taught Pallas language; Cynthia modesty;
> As fit to have encreas'd the harmony
> Of Spheares, as light of starres; She was earthes Eye:
> The sole Religious house, and Votary,
> Wth Rites not bound, but conscience. Wouldst thou All?
> She was '*Sell Boulstred*. In wch name, I call
> Up so much truth, as could I it pursue
> Might make the Fable of *Good Women* true.   (3–14)

The reticence formula enters the service of Jonson in avoiding the particulars. In fact, Jonson provides only one detail about Cecilia Bulstrode: she was a virgin in such a place as the court. But in lines 6–11, Jonson replaces the particular by a series of "outdoing" comparisons with mythological figures: she is peerless in beauty, wisdom, virtue, and piety, surpassing even the goddesses. And this commonplace rhetorical device for heightening praise is superseded in lines 12–14 by typically Jonsonian, and the highest, praise— the invocation of her name. For brevity nothing could be more effective: " '*Sell Boulstred*" by itself is the embodiment of all the virtues the preceding lines have enumerated. Calling her by her own name is a gesture of making the "fable" true.

Since the lamentation has been reduced to a half line, consolation is not made explicit, but is implied in the praise: that she was virtuous is in itself a consolation, and the exact correspondence between her name and its "truth" is in itself a reward. As is only to be expected from his classicizing of Cecilia Bulstrode, Jonson offers not a Christian vision of immortality of soul but a Roman vision of immortality of name: she will live in this epitaph, even as the good women live in Chaucer's *Legend of Good Women*. (Of course, as I have said before, the fame of Chaucer's "Good Women" is of a dubious kind.)

Through the strategy of brevity and reticence, Jonson succeeds in minimizing the topics of lamentation and consolation, which, after all, are more likely to require his personal involvement. In fact, the whole poem can be read as a treatment of the topics of commendation only. Moreover, the commendation is done chiefly through withholding particulars. The result is a highly idealized picture of Cecilia Bulstrode, hardly expounded in detail, but hyperbolically heightened by allusions to mythological figures. The personal aspects of Cecilia Bulstrode are stylized out of existence. And in that picture there can be no room for a display of Jonson's personal feelings about her, except what is implied in his reticence.

Jonson uses actual personages to people the ideal world his poems create. In his hands, these personages are re-created into exemplary pictures of vices and virtues. Cecilia Bulstrode, both in the epigram and in the epitaph, is so much idealized that she is no longer identifiable as a specific woman. She is an epitome of Vanity Fair as a court pucelle, or a paragon of virtue as a court virgin. As historical documents about Jonson and Cecilia Bulstrode, these poems do not say much. If one wants to wring more out of them, one has to learn how to decode Jonson's language of reticence, the means he uses to stylize and thus translate Cecilia Bulstrode into his re-created world.

2

Jonson's Factual Drama

Sejanus and Catiline

Jonson's only tragedies—*Sejanus* (1603) and *Catiline* (1611)—were received with general disfavor when they were first staged. *Sejanus,* as Jonson informs us, "suffer'd no lesse violence / from our people here, then the subject of it did from the rage of / the people of Rome" (Dedicatory Epistle to Lord Aubigny, 9–11). *Catiline,* he tells us, was again an abysmal failure. It fell victim to the "thick, and darke an ignorance" of an audience in "Jig-given times" (Dedicatory Epistle to the Earl of Pembroke, 1–5). The Roman pair fared little better with posterity, whom Jonson had to trust for an enlightened appreciation of his work. For Pepys in the Restoration period, *Catiline* still remained "the worst upon the stage, I mean, the least diverting, that ever I saw any."[1] And in our own times their failure as tragedies has frequently been remarked and in fact has been the focus of most critical discussions of the works.

Modern critics are quick to point out that these plays are unable to offer a tragic resolution like that of Shakespeare's Roman tragedies: instead of allowing the audience, as Hunter says, a "sense of cadence, of conclusion," or order restored, the plays leave them with an uncomfortable anticipation that there is to be yet another fruitless round of struggle for power. Critics often conclude their discussions by condemning the plays' lack of "moral vision," as, for example, Ornstein does when he finds "a void of ethical meaning at the heart of Jonson's tragedies which the great bulk of moralizing commentary only emphasizes."[2]

Seeking a cause of this alleged lack of moral vision in Jonson's tragedies, some critics blame his unimaginative, if fastidiously scholarly, handling of his historical sources.[3] They take their cue from Jonson himself, who directs the reader's attention to his extraordinary fidelity to historical facts as they are reported by antiquity, calling this fidelity "integrity of . . . story" and "truth of Argument" ("To the Readers" prefixed to *Sejanus*). They argue that his slavish adherence to historical accounts of Sejanus and Catiline prevented him from rearranging and refashioning the accounts. And the outcome is said to be a dramatized history, not a comprehensive statement about life, as poetry should be. This argument derives from no less an authority than the arch-defender of poetry Sidney: in spirit it follows closely Sidney's rhetorical condemnation of history in favor of poetry. Jonson the historian is "so tied, not to what should be but to what is, to the particular truth of things, that his example draweth no necessary consequences, and therefore a less fruitful doctrine" (*Defence of Poetry*, 89).

The issue involved in this argument is not unrelated to the epideictic poet's dual allegiance to the truth of particular things and the truth of timeless ideals: how, if at all, can Jonson interpret and fictionalize what are given as established historical facts? What does he do with "facts"? The answer throws a useful light on the epideictic method he uses in order to turn actual persons and actual events into pictures of ideals. In fact, he has made a few significant changes on Tacitus's *Annals* or Sallust's *Conspiracy of Catiline*.[4] In *Sejanus* he has suppressed the awkward fact that Livia, Drusus's wife and Sejanus's mistress, was a sister to Germanicus, making at the same time Agrippina, widow of Germanicus and the moral center of the Germanicans, much more virtuous than historical accounts of her warrant. In *Catiline*, too, he has changed historical sources for his own purposes. The first and most conspicuous change occurs in the beginning of the play, where Catiline is shown to be the spiritual heir of bloodthirsty Sulla, himself an unfair distortion of the historical *dictatore*. Jonson has also added the crucial hint of Caesar's complicity in Catiline's plot, which he has adopted from the *Historia coniurationis Catilinariae* of Constantius Felicius Durantinus. Although they are small in number, these changes strengthen the "arguments" of the plays, giving them a coherence lacking in the original accounts. By maintaining silence about Livia's genealogy, Jonson in effect enhances the moral position of the Germanicans as virtuous opponents of the vicious Tiberius. Caesar's complicity in the Catilinarian plot is almost necessary to justify the interpretation of the conspiracy as one link in the chain of events that led to the final disintegration of republican Rome. Jonson's fictionalizing tendency is as clearly at work here as it is in his poems of praise. Even while adhering faithfully to his sources, he is tending toward the creation of a highly coherent, if not idealized, picture of a world he never lived in but can understand in light of what he knows about his own world.[5]

Defined in this way, the issue raised by Jonson's Roman tragedies needs to be examined not only in comparison with the historical sources but in the context of the "moral vision" (in Ornstein's phrase) he characteristically brings to any work. These tragedies, like his comedies, are about the depraved and depraving power of fiction and disguise manipulated by a degenerate artist.[6] The tragic world of *Sejanus* and *Catiline* is not different from the comic world of *Volpone, The Alchemist,* or *Bartholomew Fair.*[7] In both worlds, civilization is threatened by the forces of disintegration and corruption, which send the comic knave to a series of disguises and the tragic villain to an endless political maneuvering. "Playacting" is not merely a metaphor but an active mode of living in these worlds: the human faculty of imagination is almost indistinguishable from the inclination to pry into others' hearts and manipulate them with the knowledge so gained. The sameness of the two worlds—comic/fictional and tragic/historical—demonstrates better than anything else the decorum of Jonson's peculiar version of the theater metaphor, through which he viewed human life both past and present: "I *have* considered, our whole life is like a *Play:* wherein every man, forgetfull of himselfe, is in travaile with expression of another. Nay, wee so insist in imitating others, as wee cannot (when it is necessary) returne to our selves" (*Discoveries, H&S* 8:597).

In his tragedies, as in his comedies and masques, Jonson examines the nature of theater—the art of play acting and play making—and the relationship between the playwright and the audience. The trope of *theatrum mundi* is so pervasive in the plays that it is difficult to avoid the conclusion that it is indeed their structural idea. The play metaphor, in its double reference to the realms of art and politics, is related to another of Jonson's favorite tropes: the medieval Renaissance analogy between the king and God the creator, or the poet-creator. The trope's identification of the king with the poet expresses the king's absolute power over his kingdom. But Jonson's use of the trope in his epigrams to King James (Epigrams 4 and 35) and his court masques suggests that he finds it a particularly fitting vehicle for his deeply held beliefs about the social functions of art. The king and the poet share the same power and obligation to create and re-create the world. The poet has the poetic power to create a golden fiction out of brazen facts, and the king has the political power to translate his ideals into reality. In terms of the play metaphor, the king is the playwright for his theater-kingdom; at the same time he is a player acting out his own script. But the play metaphor is inevitably two-edged: it can be used to represent both the ideal and the depraved ruler, both the prince acting out his ideals and the one only pretending to be an ideal ruler. And the king, with his absolute control over his kingdom, can exploit both the sinister and the educative possibilities of theater (or any art). He can erect a golden kingdom upon the leaden one, or he can destroy his kingdom with his own depravity, encompassing every member of the society in the deadly circle of a tragedy.[8]

If his court masques are an idealization of the poet-prince, Jonson's tragedies are an acknowledgment of the destructive potential of the same poet-prince. His tragic world is a masque world turned upside down. *Sejanus* and *Catiline* show the world-stage, where his worst antitheatrical fears of fiction and disguise are actualized and the morally suspect aspects of theater are exploited. It is a world where the playwright creates deceptive illusions in order to attain an absolute control over the audience, and where the audience is duped by the playwright, failing to comprehend his intentions and confusing illusion with reality. The major villains of the plays—Sejanus, Tiberius, and Catiline—are in part playwrights who plot to control their audiences (and their victims) with a godlike power, working upon their fears and desires with dramatic illusions. Through their plots they transform their society into a theater, and every member of that society into a human puppet playing out a preordained role. From that tragic theater, there is no escape except through death.

Describing the demoralized Rome under Tiberius and his minion Sejanus, Tacitus calls special attention to the tyrannous control they exercised over the words and actions of the Romans. In the universal fear of persecution, not only the common citizens but even the highest patricians turned to the informer's trade, for self-preservation, or as if infected by a plague; words, even those spoken in private, carry in their sounds as much danger as deeds do; even the walls seem to have ears. For example, Nero Caesar, Germanicus's heir, we are told, was persecuted for words he had never spoken as well as those he had spoken. For him "Even night-time was not safe. For whether he slept, or lay awake, or sighed, his wife Livia Julia told her mother Livilla, and she told Sejanus" (*Annals*, 183). Their tyranny over the mind of Rome was such that "all eyes watched for imperial commands" (*Annals*, 31), the people completely submitting themselves to the roles prescribed for them. And Tiberius, "even when he did not aim at concealment, was—by habit of nature—always hesitant, always cryptic" (*Annals*, 37).

Jonson must have found in Tacitus's account a true example of a disintegration of a society reflected in its degenerate language. In Sejanus's Rome, language, which should be "the Instrument of *Society*" (*Discoveries*, *H&S* 8:621), is turned into an instrument of alienation, a handle of tyranny. By misinterpreting others' words and actions, by forcing his own version of truth upon others, Tiberius exacts from their mouths what he will have. He becomes the author of their speech, their action, and indeed their fate. He turns into a tyrannical playwright for that great theater Rome.

The play appropriately begins with an introduction into the theater-

within-the-theater by those who represent the old ideals. At the very beginning of the play, Sabinus and Silius analyze the essentially theatrical nature of
Tiberius's tyranny—his authorial control of Rome—observing the sinister
similarities between theater and Tiberian court. Sabinus's first speech is a
negative definition of Tiberian politicians as "inginers":

> wee are no good inginers.
> We want the fine arts, & their thriving use,
> Should make us grac'd, or favour'd of the times:
> We have no shift of faces, no cleft tongues,
> No soft, and glutinous bodies, that can sticke,
> Like snailes, on painted walls; or, on our brests,
> Creep up, to fall, from that proud height, to which
> We did by slaverie, not by service, clime.   (1.4–11)

Statecraft is stagecraft, politics a contest of theatricality. The fear and
contempt of theater—its suspect capacity to deceive and manipulate the
audience through disguise and spectacle—expressed in these lines are in turn
a criticism of Tiberius's statecraft. If Tiberius and Sejanus are "inginers,"
their followers are puppets moving on their masters' cue:

> These can lye,
> Flatter, sweare, forsweare, deprave, informe,
> Smile, and betray; make guilty men; then beg
> The forfeit lives, to get the livings; cut
> Mens throates with whisprings; sell to gaping sutors
> The emptie smoake, that flyes about the Palace;
> Laugh, when their patron laughes; sweat, when he sweates;
> Be hot, and cold with him; change every moode,
> Habit, and garbe, as often as he varies;
> Observe him, as his watch observes his clocke;   (1.27–36)

This initial perception is underscored throughout the play by the play-
making and playacting activities of Tiberius and Sejanus. And their theatricality and its ultimate aim—that they dissemble in order to manipulate—
are understood and exposed by choric observers like Arruntius, Silius, Lepidus, and Sabinus, who try to detach themselves from the degenerate games
of politics. Tiberius, with Sejanus, presents three playlets of his own devising
at three crucial points of the play—in acts 1, 3, and 5—before the Senate.
The scene before the Senate in act 1 shows Tiberius in the role of a magnani-
mous ruler with Sejanus assisting him as a loyal servant. The total disparity
between his words and his intentions is so obvious that it evokes the image of
an actor, an image which emphasizes his hypocrisy. The very presence at his
side of Sejanus the arch-flatterer, whose statue he is now consecrating to
Pompey's Theater, gives a lie to his only "lip-good" pronouncements against

flattery. It is an act "Rarely dissembled" (1.395), and its significance is pointedly observed by Silius: it is a death knell for even the remnants of the old Rome, which was free from flattery, the need of flattery, or rather the need of dissembling to be free from flattery:

> "Men are deceiv'd, who thinke there can be thrall
> "Beneath a vertuous prince. Wish'd liberty
> "Ne'er lovelier looks, then under such a crowne.
> But, when his grace is meerely but lip-good,
> And, that no longer, then aires himselfe
> Abroad in publique, there, to seeme to shun
> The strokes, and stripes of flatterers, which within
> Are lechery unto him, and so feed
> His brutish sense with their afflicting sound,
> As (dead to vertue) he permits himselfe
> Be carried like a pitcher, by the eares,
> To every act of vice: this is a case
> Deserves our feare, and doth presage the nigh,
> And close approach of bloud and tyranny.   (1.407–20)

The old Rome, in *Sejanus,* is indeed a thing of the past. It lives on only in the handful of Germanican party members, and in their fierce idealization of Germanicus as the culmination and the last bloom of the old republican Rome, as the one in whom

> POMPEI's dignitie
> The innocence of CATO, CAESAR's spirit,
> Wise BRUTUS temperance, and every vertue,
> Which, parted unto others, gave them name,
> Flow'd mixt in him.   (1.150–54)

The chillingly effective "painting scene," inset between Tiberius's first and the second public appearances, shows that the close alliance between dissimulation, flattery, and tyranny affects not only Tiberius's court but also his own private house. The picture of Livia, Tiberius's daughter-in-law, being whitened, smoothened, and beautified by the pandering hand of Eudemus, even while being moved to adultery and murder of her husband by his no less pandering tongue, is an emblem of the Tiberian corruption. And the extent of that corruption can be measured by the celerity and casualness with which Livia embraces her new role as a partner in Sejanus's plot. Creating and shifting roles are the rule and become as easy as mixing fucus with poison, mask with face, political scheme with love intrigue, and private vice with public evil.

Tiberius's mastery in public rhetoric—the glib and oily art to speak and purpose not—becomes in his second public appearance a tyranny over the other Romans' language. In act 3, when he appears before the Senate after his son Drusus's death, Tiberius again creates confusion among the senators by exalting Germanicus's sons and declaring his intention to retire. He is indeed a "SPHINX," as Arruntius says, whom only those "OEDIPUS inough" could understand (3.64–65). His exploitation of the delusive possibilities of rhetoric is accompanied by a deliberate misinterpretation of others' words and deeds in conformity with predetermined significances. The close alliance between tyranny and misinterpretation is exposed and denounced in turn by Silius and Cordus in their trials.[9]

Called forward for indictment on fabricated charges, and deprived of the protection of the law, Silius denounces Tiberius's fraudulent interpretation of trial laws as "worse then violence" (3.209). The equation between linguistic control and political control Silius makes in the denunciation summarizes accurately the nature of Tiberius's tyranny. The tyrant appropriates language entirely to himself, denying his victims the right to control the meanings of their words. The law itself, which should provide a defense against such tyranny, is taught to speak the tyrant's pleasures. Tiberius is able to maintain his absolute power over Rome through his "Furious enforcing, most unjust presuming, / Malicious, and manifold applying, / Foul wresting, and impossible construction" (3.227–29) of the words of the Romans.

The trial that follows of Cordus the historian for treasonable and seditious writing makes it once more clear how effective a tool of tyranny misinterpretation is. Afer, Tiberius's instrument for the occasion, makes the accusation that Cordus, with his "licentious pen" (3.404), deliberately compares men of the present with those of previous history—a practice that "is most strangely invective. / Most full of spight, and insolent upbraiding" (3.399–400). And Cordus's absolute denial that he tries to mean more than what he writes is not only a defense of language but an attack on Tiberius's Rome, where anything can be made to mean anything, where, as Arruntius laments later in the play, "Nothing hath priviledge 'gainst the violent eare" (4.311):

> all matter,
> Nay all occasion pleaseth. Mad-mens rage,
> The idlenesse of drunkards, womens nothing,
> Jesters simplicity, all, all is good
> That can be catch'd at. (4.314–18)

Tiberius's art of tyranny through deceptive public rhetoric and misinterpretation of others' language reaches its fine pitch of psychological torture in his offstage performance in act 5, when he strikes down Sejanus with a carefully composed letter. And his art of equivocation and dissimulation this time is employed to create a fear of misinterpretation among the Romans. His contradictory letters, which he has sent to various Romans in the last two acts, alienate them from his true intention, even while subjugating them with fear and doubt, and making them into human puppets. He praises Sejanus in one letter and dispraises him in another. The Romans are left "Divided, and suspended, all uncertaine" (4.422), like Laco, who says:

> These forked tricks, I understand 'hem not,
> Would he would tell us whom he loves, or hates,
> That we might follow, without feare, or doubt.   (4.423–25)

About Tiberius's intention to overthrow Sejanus, even Lepidus can only guess:

> These cross points
> Of varying letters, and opposing *Consuls,*
> Mingling his honours, and his punishments,
> Feigning now ill, now well, raising SEJANUS,
> And then depressing him, (as now of late
> In all reports we have it) cannot be
> Emptie of practice: 'Tis TIBERIUS arte.   (4.447–53)

The dehumanizing effects of the fear of misinterpretation he deliberately arouses throughout the two acts are reflected in the senators' puppetlike movement while his final letter is being read. Each time he revises what he has said about Sejanus in previous lines with *but*s, *yet*s, and *though*s, subtly changing equivocal praise to explicit indictment, the senators, one by one, fall away from Sejanus, like crawling vines (in Arruntius's words), little constant in the face of the whirling wind. And when they join in the "beastly rage of the people" to tear Sejanus apart, the process of their dehumanization is complete.

But this play's concern, the tragedy of an imperial theater presided over by a degenerate playwright, finds its most effective expression in the identification of Tiberius with Fortune. Tiberius's obsessive concern with his own and others' language springs from his lust for a godlike control over his own and others' lives.[10] Throughout the play, his tyrannical rule over Rome is directly and indirectly associated with the rule of Fortune, as the arbitress of men's fate, over the world-stage. The resemblance between him and Fortune is especially striking in Arruntius's description in act 4:

> he lives,
> (Acting his *tragedies* with a *comick* face)
> Amid'st his rout of *Chaldee's:* spending houres,
> Dayes, weekes, and months, in the unkind abuse
> Of grave *astrologie,* to the bane of men,
> Casting the scope of men's nativities,
> And having found aught worthy in their fortune,

> Kill, or precipitate them in the sea,
> And boast, he can mocke fate.   (4.378–86)

This description occurs, significantly, when Tiberius is about to present the conclusion of his masterpiece in *de casibus* pattern, the drama of Sejanus's rise and fall.

The drama is an illustration of the destructive power such a poet-ruler could have over his own empire. In fact, Tiberius's playacting and play making is directed against not only his enemies but also his crafty favorite, to whom he lends his Fortune-like power, and who believes "Jove but my equal, Caesar but my second" (5.264). In the first half of the play, the master in the "tyrants' art" of deceit and machination appears to be Sejanus rather than Tiberius. He entertains a "design" (2.382) to work upon the emperor's fears in order to bind him in a puppetlike subjection to himself: he intends

>   to present the shapes
> Of dangers, greater then they are (like late,
> Or early shadowes) and, sometimes, to faine
> Where there are none, onley, to make him feare;   (2.384–87)

Indeed, the authorial control seems to be in his rather than Tiberius's hand when he stages the trial of Silius and Cordus, assigning Tiberius the role of an innocent prince and literally handing the script to the accusers of his own creation: "Here be your notes," he tells Varro, "what points to touch at; read: / Bee cunning in them. AFER ha's them too" (3.7–8). He seems to be something more than a playwright for Tiberius's theater: he has the power to control others' lives as a "court-god," "well applied / With sacrifice of knees, of crookes, and cringe" (1.203–4); as the "soule of *Rome,* / The empires life, and voice of CAESARS world!" (2.55–56); as a gigantic pruner of some primaeval forest-garden, lopping down "the loftie Cedar of the world, / GERMANICUS . . . DRUSUS, that upright Elme . . . SILIUS and SABINUS, two strong Oakes . . . besides, those other shrubs," and "re-plant[ing]" their younger "branches" (5.242–46); as a destroyer as powerful as some natural disaster like a "tempest" (5.624); or as a Titanic rebel heaving "mountain upon mountain" against gods, driving the universe to the brink of total disintegration (4.266–71).

Sejanus's false security as "a master in his mysterie" (4.184) reaches a ridiculous height in his swelling hyperboles:

>   Great, and high,
> The world knowes only two, that's *Rome,* and I.
> My roofe receives me not; 'tis aire I tread:
> And, each step, I feele my'advanced head
> Knocke out a starre in heav'n!   (5.5–9)

When he slaps the averted face of Fortune, he seems indeed to have gained a mastery over his fortune.

In true *de casibus* fashion, Tiberius reasserts his authorial power by striking down Sejanus when the minion's mastery over the tyrant and Fortune seems most complete. The minion's fall confirms the suspicion of Tiberius's opponents like Lepidus that Sejanus is only a "creature" shaped by Tiberius with his subtle art. He is a player acting out a role predetermined by Tiberius, even when he believes he is his own author. As Marco, Sejanus's replacement in Tiberius' favor, is well aware, Tiberius is the Fortune for the world of Rome. He uses that world as a stage for acting out his blind will, raising minions and pulling them down again as he pleases.

Sejanus's fall does not bring Tiberius's drama to an end. Instead, it emphasizes Tiberius's and by extension Fortune's destructive power. A society ruled with degenerate statecraft is a hostage to Fortune, who "plies her sports" still (5.888). The author of Sejanus's rise and fall will devise another scene of violent rise and fall. One minion's destruction is another's ascent. Arruntius the satiric observer prophesies that Rome will witness another such drama, one of a different hero and of a greater destructive power:

> I prophesie out of this *Senates* flatterie,
> That this new fellow, MARCO, will become
> A greater prodigie in *Rome,* then he
> That now is falne. (5.750–53)

The tragic vision of life that found the proper material for drama in the Sejanus episode operates in *Catiline* with the same grim intensity. *Catiline* is, as W. F. Bolton and Jane F. Gardner point out in a different context, "a reworking of the preoccupations and techniques" of the earlier tragedy *Sejanus.*[11] Catiline's Rome is yet to become the imperial Rome of Tiberius and Sejanus. But Jonson finds in it the same ruthless laws of politics and the same oppressive hypocrisy that were at once the cause and the effect of the moral disintegration of Tiberius's Rome. In both Romes, Jonson finds an amoral conspiracy forestalled by such means as have few other moral justifications than that they preserve the *status quo* in order to perpetuate the same corruption that has engendered such a conspiracy in the first place. Like *Sejanus, Catiline* is a tragedy of a society that through its own corruption is turned into a theater for a contest of degenerate stagecraft.

The beginning of *Catiline* is the most significant of the few departures Jonson makes from his sources. None of the sources—Sallust, Cicero, Dio Cassius, and Plutarch—mention Catiline's midnight reception of Sylla's ghost, which locates the play within the tradition of Senecan tragedy. Sylla's ghost returns from the dead to hasten Rome to her destruction:

Do'st thou not feele me, Rome? not yet? Is night
So heavy on thee, and my weight so light?

      . . . . .

What sleepe is this doth seize thee, so like death,
And is not it? Wake, feele her, in my breath:
Behold, I come, sent from the Stygian sound,
As a dire vapor, that had cleft the ground,
T'ingender with the night, and blast the day;
Or like a pestilence, that should display
Infection through the world: which, thus, I doe.   (1.1–15)

And he chooses Catiline as his spiritual heir who will carry out for him the
task of destruction, infusing him with his own dark spirit:

PLUTO be at thy councells; and into
Thy darker bosome enter SYLLA's spirit:
All, that was mine, and bad, thy brest inherit.
Alas, how weake is that, for CATILINE!
Did I but say (vain voice!) all that was mine?
All, that the GRACCHI, CINNA, MARIUS would;
What now, had I a body againe, I could,
Coming from hell; what Fiends would wish should be;
And HANNIBAL could not have wish'd to see:
Think thou, and practice.   (1.16–25)

Neither the reception nor the representation of Sylla as ultimately responsible for the destruction of the Roman Republic is wholly true to historical
facts. But the effect Jonson creates with this change is very much in line with
Sallust's interpretation of the Catilinarian conspiracy. Sallust's purpose in
writing *Conspiracy of Catiline* is not only to record a criminal enterprise
"unprecedented in itself and fraught with unprecedented dangers to Rome"
(Sallust, 177), but to examine that particular crime as a link in the chain of
events that at once caused and manifested the Roman degeneration from
republican virtue to imperial depravity. His preface to *Conspiracy of Catiline*
is filled with regrets about the vanished and vanishing virtues of republican
Rome, a society betrayed by its own military successes and the economic
prosperity that followed them. From the vantage point of 35 B.C., Sallust
could recognize that the apparent benefits of Rome's success in her imperial
ambition were a curse in disguise. In the early Rome, he says, both in peace
and war,

virtue was held in high esteem. The closest unity prevailed, and avarice was a
thing almost unknown. Justice and righteousness were upheld not so much
by law as by natural instinct. They quarrelled and fought with their country's
foes; between themselves the citizens contended for honour. In making

offerings to the gods they spared no expense; at home they lived frugally and never betrayed a friend. By combining boldness in war with fair dealing when peace was restored, they protected themselves and the state. (181)

Hard work and justice brought Rome prosperity; but

it was then that fortune turned unkind and confounded all her enterprises. To the men who had so easily endured toil and peril, anxiety and adversity, the leisure and riches which are generally regarded as so desirable proved a burden and curse. Growing love of money, and the lust for power which followed it, engendered every kind of evil. Avarice destroyed honour, integrity, and every other virtue, and instead taught men to be proud and cruel, to neglect religion, and to hold nothing too sacred to sell. Ambition tempted many to be false, to have one thought hidden in their hearts, another ready on their tongues, to become a man's friend or enemy not because they judged him worthy or unworthy but because they thought it would pay them, and to put on the semblance of virtues that they had not. At first these vices grew slowly and sometimes met with punishment; later on, when the disease spread like a plague, Rome changed: her government, once so just and admirable, became harsh and unendurable. (182–83)

Sylla and Catiline were respectively the seed and the offspring of this general corruption; the one ushered in an era of "universal robbery and pillage" (182), and the other was incited to a crime by "the corruption of a society plagued by two opposite but equally disastrous vices—love of luxury and love of money" (178). Sylla's destructive urge, in Sallust's view, was the same urge that actuated Catiline and hurried Rome along to her moral destruction. By introducing Sylla's ghost at the beginning of the play, Jonson turns a tragedy of an individual into a tragedy of a society, identifying Catiline as something of a puppet not only of his own vices but also of those enervating the whole society. Act I of *Catiline,* which begins with the infusion of Sylla's spirit into Catiline, and through Catiline into other members of Roman society, appropriately ends with the Chorus lamenting the fate of Rome defeated by her own prosperity:

> *Rome,* now, is Mistris of the whole
> World, sea, and land, to either pole;
> And even that fortune will destroy
> The power that made it: she doth joy
> So much in plentie, wealth, and ease,
> As, now, th'excess is her disease.
>
> . . . . .
>
> Hence comes that wild, and vast expence,
> That hath enforc'd *Romes* vertue, thence,
> Which simple poverty first made:
>
> . . . . .

> Such ruine of her manners *Rome*
> Doth suffer now, as shee's become
> (Without the gods it soone gaine-say)
> Both her own spoiler, and owne prey.
>
> (1.545–50, 573–75, 583–86)

Jonson maintains throughout the play this initial identification of Cati-line's career as a mirror of Roman degeneration. The historical Catiline, who was interested in sound reform measures like redistribution of wealth to the impoverished nobility, is barely recognizable in Jonson's Catiline, who complains chiefly about the private wrong he has suffered at the hands of new men like Cicero (1.326–73). Catiline in Jonson's play is an embodiment of the disintegrating forces of Roman society: he excites in people around him the forces of violence, darkness, and death, which a society with deteriorated moral moorings is powerless to resist.

When the play begins, Catiline has already dispensed with the most fundamental units of the society—family and religion—as a filicide, uxoricide, fratricide, perpetrator of incest, and rapist of a Vestal virgin. And the analogy between the family and the city, which he uses in his first speech of the play, tells us that his rebellion against Rome is an act against his own mother, against her womb, against the origin of his very being. It is nothing else than an expression of his death wish, Titanic in its violence but infantile in its desperation:

> It is decree'd. Nor shall thy Fate, o *Rome,*
> Resist my vow. Though hills were set on hills,
> And seas met seas, to guard thee; I would through:
> I, plough up rocks, steepe as the *Alpes,* in dust;
> And lave the *Tyrrhene* waters, into clouds;
> But I would reach thy head, thy head, proud citie.
>
> . . . . .
>
> I will, hereafter, call her step-dame, ever.
> If shee can loose her nature, I can loose
> My pietie; and in her stony entrailes
> Dig me a seate: where, I will live, againe,
> The labour of her wombe, and be a burden,
> Weightier than all the prodigies, and monsters,
> That shee hath teem'd with, since shee first knew MARS.
>
> (1.73–78, 91–97)

By breaking familial ties, Catiline tries to attain a godlike freedom from the laws of humankind. "Freedom" and "liberty" are the catchwords most often used among his confederates. But their freedom is a freedom to destroy: they want to restore

>   the dayes
> Of SYLLA's sway, when the free sword took leave
> To act all that it would!
>   And was familiar
> With entrailes as our Augures!
>   Sonnes kild fathers,
> Brothers their brothers.
>   And had price, and praise.
> All hate had licence given it: all rage reines.   (1.229–34)

And through their freedom to slaughter and destroy, they want to go beyond the plane of all living things. Catiline's promise to "stick my ORESTILLA, there, amongst" stars is not just a piece of rhetorical extravagance (1.127). It is a vow against all humanity, a vow to make it "a crime inough, that they [have] lives" (1.244), and a vow which is, fittingly, sealed with a human sacrifice (1.485–98).

But by a fearful logic of things, Catiline's autochthonous freedom places him at the mercy of the contingencies of relationships. As Thomas Greene observes, in the Jonsonian world, one who cannot hold a "centered self" must needs travel, throwing himself into the flux and mutability of the world-stage to act and to be acted upon in turn through endless shifts of disguises.[12] Catiline's plot against Rome begins with an illusion that he can remake the world into a theater of his own and create human puppets serving his own pleasures. The language he uses in the organizational meeting with his new wife Aurelia is charged with theatrical metaphors: he asks her "to put on / Like habites with my selfe" (1.130–31), and to create a troupe of lady puppets in "a fashion / Of freedome, and community" (1.176–77), while he himself works on some with a picture of bright future, some with lust, some with desperation, some with revenge, some with money, and all with self-love. Several vices need several gratifications. He has to do

> With many men, and many natures. Some,
> That must be blowne, and sooth'd; as LENTULUS,
>
>   . . . . .
>   Then, bold CETHEGUS,
> Whose valour I have turn'd into his poison,
> And prais'd so into daring, as he would
> Goe on upon the gods, kisse lightening, wrest
> The engine from the CYCLOPS'S . . .
>
>   . . . . .
> When I would bid him move.   (1.132–46)

The whole affair is a setup knowingly put on, and they are a pair of gods in disguise playing the mean roles of humans, roles which,

Like one of JUNO'S, or of JOVE'S disguises,
　　　　 . . . will as soone,
When things succeed, be throwne by, or let fall,
As is a vaile put off, a visor chang'd,
Or the *scene* shifted, in our *theaters*—　　　　(1.181–85)

Catiline's insistent theatrical metaphors turn their political plot into a dramatic plot, and himself into a playwright with an absolute control over his characters. But what he has forgotten is that by turning his world into a theater he turns himself into a player as well as a playwright. And the law of the theater, cosmic and otherwise, is such that without detached "spectators" a player must act only with other players, and in Crites' words, "no one [sees] the motion, but the motion" (*Cynthia's Revels* 1.5.64). The puppet who believes himself to be the sole puppeteer is often the most foolish puppet of all. The success of a theatrical maneuver is always contingent on there being no countermaneuver of a superior theatrical skill. Even as Mosca outfoxes Volpone, even as Face outdoes Subtle in subtlety, even as Tiberius outclasses Sejanus in political cunning, or even as Fortune outplays the historical Tiberius in underhanded treachery, so does Cicero outwit Catiline in his plotting. Cicero, a superior artist, is able to use Catiline's art for his own purpose.

Cicero is presented throughout the play as a master in the mystery of governorship. In Cato's words, he knows

His tides, his currents; how to shift his sailes;
What shee will bear in foule, what in faire weathers,
Where her springs are, her leakes; and how to stop'em;
What sands, what shelves, what rocks doe threaten her;
The forces, and the natures of all winds,
Gusts, stormes, and tempests; when her keele ploughs hell,
And deck knocks heaven.　　　　(3.67–73)

But Cicero is no Cato, who is nothing if not an embodiment of unyielding integrity. Pragmatism and opportunism characterize his statecraft as much as they do Catiline's political maneuvering. He dissembles, flatters, and works upon others' vanities. His essential resemblance to Catiline in his political opportunism is made recognizable in act 3, when he first appears in the play. Like Catiline, he puts on "habits" with many men. In order to win Curius over to his side, he praises Fulvia, the younger man's mistress, to whose double-dealing he owes the discovery of Catiline's plot:

Here is a lady, that hath got the start,
In pietie, of us all; and, for whose vertue,
I could almost turne lover, again: but that

TERENTIA would be jealous. What an honor
Hath shee achieved to her selfe! What voices,
Titles, and loud applauses will pursue her,
Through every street! What windores will be fill'd
To shoot eyes at her! . . .

. . . . . .

'Tis no shame, to follow
The better precedent. She shewes you, CURIUS.

(3.341–48, 358–59)

But what he really thinks of the character of this self-appointed informant is evident from his soliloquy after her departure with her lover:

O *Rome,* in what a sicknesse art thou fall'n!

. . . . . .

. . . that the first symptomes
Of such maladie, should not rise out
From any worthy member, but a base
And common strumpet, worthlesse to be nam'd
A haire, or part of thee? (3.438–52)

Bribery is not unknown to him: he bribes Antonius, the other consul, into silence and the Allobroges into cooperation in defeating Catiline. Evidently his governorship includes adroit use of such usual tools of political machination as expediency, dissimulation, and duplicity. In fact, throughout the play there are nagging hints that Cicero exaggerates the real threat of Catiline's conspiracy in order to advance his own political career. Caesar, for example, is prepared to interpret Cicero's loud declamation against Catiline as a stratagem to gain popularity. To the unsuspecting Catulus he suggests:

Doe you not tast
An art, that is so common? Popular men,
They must create strange monsters, and then quell'hem:
To make their artes seem something. Would you have
Such an HERCULEAN actor in the scene,
And not his HYDRA? (3.95–100)

What distinguishes Cicero from Catiline is that he is equipped with a superior ability to see into men's minds, a matchless oratorical skill to work upon men's affections, and above all the obvious moral justification that his political maneuvering is for the salvation of the state. Indeed, Cicero's effectiveness as a politician comes from his pose as a disinterested observer of the corrupt Rome of Catiline, a society bent on its own destruction. In his election speech before the Senate, he emphasizes that he is a "novus homo"— a new man not only in the sense that he is an "upstart" (2.119), or "A mushroome? one of yesterday" (2.136), as his enemies understand him to be, but a man free from the vices of the old nobility as well as from their "urnes . . . dusty moniments . . . broken images of ancestors / Wanting an eare, or nose" (3.14–16). He is a man who has made his fame through virtue and merit alone. And with that argument of virtue, he is able to enlist the support of the Senate, already panicked at the prospect of another civil war, and to condemn Catiline successfully.

Although Catiline's plot to turn the whole world of Rome into a theater of destruction falls ineffectual before Cicero, *Catiline* is not a play about the forces of stability finally triumphing over the forces of disintegration. History tells us that through his political maneuvers, Cicero only perpetuated the corruption of Rome; the city had already produced Catiline, and it was destined to fall into civil wars waged among Caesar, Pompey, Octavius, and Antonius. Such historical perspective is detectable first in the identification of Catiline as the proper heir of Sylla, then in the tainted means Cicero uses to foil Catiline's plot, and finally in the implication that Caesar, not Catiline, is the true author of the conspiracy. In the ending of *Catiline*, as in that of *Sejanus*, Fortune still "plies her sports," driving the depraved world-stage to disintegration. The grim picture of the destroyed Catiline, "not with the face / Of any man, but of publique ruine" (5.642–43), presages the catastrophes yet to come.

3

Fact and Fiction in Jonson's Epideictic Poetry

Understanding Jonson's poetry requires particular attention to his divided loyalties to two distinct ideas of poetry. In *Discoveries* and elsewhere, he espouses the Aristotelian doctrine that poetry is generically fiction, writing that poetry is "an Art of imitation, or faining," and that the poet "fayneth and formeth a fable, and writes things like Truth. For, the Fable and Fiction is (as it were) the forme and Soule of any Poeticall worke, or *Poem*" (*Discoveries, H&S* 8:635).[1] Yet, for the tragic plots of his two Roman plays—*Sejanus* and *Catiline*—Jonson depended on the authority of verifiable historical facts, or, as he calls it, the "truth of Argument."[2] Jonson's oscillation between the two ideas of poetry—poetry as fictive representation and poetry as factual representation—is most evident in his epideictic poetry.[3] Some tension between fact and fiction is inherent in the genre of epideictic poetry, which takes its root in history, but in some of Jonson's poems of praise the generic tension becomes an explicit concern: he constantly emphasizes his honesty in praising but at the same time admits that he has created highly idealized images of human nature. The conflict between his alternating impulses toward fact and fiction is made transparent and finally becomes a part of the poem's signification. In some of his other poems of praise, Jonson attempts to develop textual strategies that would accommodate his two impulses: he strives to create a vivid impression of factuality and particularity for his idealized and generalized images of human nature.

Dreaming the ultimate dream of a Renaissance Humanist, Jonson said to Drummond of Hawthornden that "he heth a minde to be a churchman, & so he might have favour to make one Sermon to the King, he careth not what y^{r}after sould befall him, for he would not flatter though he saw Death" (*Conversations, H&S* 1:141.330–33). Fidelity to fact; martyrlike integrity in speech. These are precisely the qualities that he represents himself to have in his poems of praise. Indeed, one of the most forceful devices of suasion he uses in his poetry is his self-characterization as an honest man. In an epistle to Katherine, Lady Aubigny, the wife of one of his most bounteous patrons (*Forest* 13), Jonson portrays himself as a solitary lover of truth and virtue, who for that love is persecuted by the "turning world" (64) mostly populated with those who buy and sell praises for gold. He speaks of the difficulty of praising in a world where persons worthy of praise are as rare as honest praisers:

> 'Tis growne almost a danger to speake true
>   Of any good minde, now: There are so few.
> The bad, by number, are so fortified,
>   As what th'have lost t[o]'expect, they dare deride.
> So both the prais'd, and praisers suffer: Yet,
>   For others ill, ought none their good forget.
> I, therefore, who profess my selfe in love
>   With every virtue, whersoere it move,
> And howsoever; as I am at fewd
>   With sinne and vice, though with a throne endew'd;
>   . . . . .
> I, *Madame,* am become your praiser.   (1–10, 21)

Honest praising in circumstances such as these lines describe is a sure sign of virtue, virtue Jonson shares with the person he praises. And appropriately, Lady Aubigny is praised in the poem for her constancy, which keeps her "farre from the maze of custome, error, strife" (60).[4] His self-characterization as an honest praiser is in turn validated by the dignified simplicity and the urbane yet earnest tone of the language used in his praise, which Wesley Trimpi has identified as characteristic of Jonsonian "plain style." By creating the impression of one talking to a friend not only intimately and candidly but also with discernment, the language Jonson uses renders his praise more credible and his advice more persuasive.[5]

But the epideictic poet cannot entirely escape the common censure of "flattery" by insisting on his moral integrity. The very nature of the world he claims he defies makes it virtually impossible for him to describe things as they are. Jonson too admits that he has not always been faithful to facts: dedicating the *Epigrammes* to William Herbert, Third Earl of Pembroke, he says, "If I have praised, unfortunately, any one, that doth not deserve; or, if all answere not, in all numbers, the pictures I have made of them: I hope it will be forgiven me, that they are no ill pieces, though they be not like the persons" (21–25). Some of his poems of praise are not "like the persons" but "pictures" he has made of them, not facts but deliberate fiction made out of the facts. And since they are not factual representations, they should not be judged by their likeness to "the persons" or their strict fidelity to facts. They should be judged, he suggests, by his skill in shaping poetic fiction.

In "To My Muse" (*Epigrammes* 65), his strongest self-rebuke for fabricating fictions, Jonson shows his awareness of the perilous resemblance of poetic fiction to deception and flattery. In an outburst of apparent self-disgust, he says to his muse:

> Away, and leave me, thou thing most abhord,
>   That hast betray'd me to a worthlesse lord;
> Made me commit most fierce idolatrie
>   To a great image through thy luxurie.
>
>   · · · · ·
>
> With me thou leav'st an happier *Muse* then thee,
>   And which thou brought'st me, welcome povertie;
> Shee shall instruct my after-thoughts to write
>   Things manly, and not smelling parasite.   (1–4, 11–14)

But a justification of poetic fiction and its dangerous power to turn a "worthlesse lord" into "a great image" soon follows. He says to his about-to-be banished muse: "But I repent me: Stay. Who e're is rais'd / For worth he has not, He is tax'd, not prais'd" (15–16). Jonson's poetic fiction is different from lies or flattery. Since he has praised the lord for what he must be, not for what he is, his overpraise is a covert "taxing," not flattery. With this claim, as William E. Cain observes, the "crisis in reference" revealed in the first four lines of the poem, when the poet acknowledges a disjunction between his language of praise and the man he praises, is resolved: "the poet's rhetoric may fail to apply truly to the man that he praises, but this no longer suggests a crisis in reference. Instead, the failure in reference exposes and censures the undeserving man; even when the poet's praise fails to refer accurately, it still serves to measure worth by calling attention to the distinction between praise and merit. While the poet's praise may fail to find a proper referent, it succeeds in revealing the man who does not deserve such praise."[6] Implicit in the claim is the idea that deviations from historical/biographical facts can be justified insofar as they serve the end of moral edification.

Of course, the justification is conventional in that it diverts one's attention to the criterion of moral utility from that of fidelity to factual truth. Sidney uses the same argument in his *Defence of Poetry*. And Erasmus offers the same apology for his eulogies of princes: he declares that "no other way of correcting a prince is so efficacious as presenting, in the guise of flattery, the pattern of a really good prince."7 The educative function of fiction (in this case, overpraise) relies heavily on the ambiguous dynamic of the relation between fact and fiction. To the person overpraised, the undeserved praise will be a form of admonition; receiving such praise will be for him an occasion for self-reflection and possibly for self-reformation. For the general audience, the "great image" of a lord will function as a form of instruction. It will assure them that there *is* a pattern of virtue in this world and will inspire them to emulate and imitate the pattern. Fiction, then, will have historical significance for both audiences. What is offered as a covert exhortation, or what is believed (if only in part) by the audiences, not what has happened, will become the basis for future action, the historical determinant. The poet can indeed reform the "worthlesse lord" into "a great image." In this sense fiction works as fact, and becomes fact. But obviously the success of this educational scheme depends not on the poet or his aim in (over)praising but on the audiences. Only when the audiences reform themselves in conformity with the praise will the overpraise cease to be a lie. Only the audiences can turn a lie into a moral lesson, and fiction into fact.

In this reproach to his muse, one might detect some ambivalence in Jonson's attitude toward fiction. The very fact that he reminds the reader of the disparity between the actual person and the artistic representation of him or her bespeaks some uneasiness about fiction. It reveals the same kind of suspicion of fiction that Sidney tried to dispel in his *Defence,* and that William Nelson diagnoses as "a persistent reluctance to accept the artistic composition of verities as equivalent to the representation of verity, even such inadequate representation as lies within the power of a historian."8 In the first fourteen lines of the poem, the distinction between falsehood and the element of fiction that inevitably enters a poem of any kind is blurred. For Jonson, whatever fiction there is in his poems of praise is either an "unfortunate" error in his judgment or his muse's act of betrayal. Poetry, like Sirens' music, lures him to a shoal of moral destruction. The moral efficacy of fiction, which for Sidney is the triumph of poetry, is offered by Jonson to the audience, but above all to himself, as a justification. The same attitude appears again in his "Epistle to Master John Selden" (*Underwood* 14). Promising Selden a just appreciation of his book, Jonson says,

> I confesse (as every Muse hath err'd,
> And mine not least) I have too oft preferr'd
> Men past their termes, and prais'd some names too much,
> But 'twas with purpose to have made them such.   (19–22)

Nevertheless, this apology is nothing if not a valediction to fictional elements in his praise. Immediately after, these lines follow:

> Since, being deceiv'd, I turne a sharper eye
> Upon my selfe, and aske to whom? and why?
> And what I write? And vexe it many dayes
> Before men get a verse: much lesse a Praise;
> So that my Reader is assur'd, I now
> Meane what I speake: and still will keepe that Vow.   (23–28)

His overpraise failed to perform its expected educative function. Hence the reassertion of the value of factual truth and of the due care and patience of epideictic composition. The reader is reassured that there will be an exact correspondence between what he says and what he means. There will be no exhortation in the guise of flattery. And the reader is more likely than otherwise to give credence to the poet's "Vow," because it is accompanied with a frank admission of past errors and an affirmation (in lines 23–26) that praise is an act of judgment: writing a poem of praise involves a close scrutiny not only of the addressee's merit but also of the poet's motive in praising.

Jonson uses here his open admission that some of his praises were in part fiction as a means to assure the reader of his honesty in praising, that is, the factuality of his poem. And this juxtaposition of an admission of fictionality and an assertion of fidelity to factual truth is Jonson's characteristic modification of Renaissance defenses of poetic fiction.

Factual representation and artistic representation had been sharply distinguished by Sir Philip Sidney in his *Defence of Poetry,* itself in part a response to the notion that truth is truth of fact, an idea which is responsible for the association of fiction with falsehood. Sidney accordingly contests the idea by differentiating between lies and fiction, between lying as deception and lying as asserting something other than factual truth; as he says of the poet, "though he recounts things not true, yet because he telleth them not for true, he lieth not. . . . so think I none so simple would say that Aesop lied in the tales of his beasts; for who thinks that Aesop writ it for actually true were well worthy to have his name chronicled among the beasts he writeth of" (102–3).

Sidney's main defense of poetic fiction is built upon that differentiation. He claims that although fiction is not factual truth, it nevertheless is truth in some special sense. In order to prove the superiority of the truth of fiction over the truth of fact, he sets poetry against history, arguing that history's very adherence to facts undermines its power to lead men to "well-doing," the "ending end" of any kind of learning. The historian, "so tied . . . to the particular truth of things," is unable to reveal "the general reason of things" (85). And "bound to tell things as things were," he must give us examples of dubious moral value (88). He must show human nature with all its inconsistencies, and the world with all its horrors. Thus "the historian, being captived to the truth of a foolish world, is many times a terror from well-doing and an encouragement to unbridled wickedness" (90). The poet, by contrast, may invent a "golden" world, which is free from all the ambiguities and contradictions of the "brazen" world of the historian, and in which virtue always triumphs. He "ever setteth virtue so out in her best colours, making Fortune her well-waiting handmaid, that one must needs be enamoured of her," and "of the contrary part, if evil men come to the stage, they ever go out . . . so manacled as they little animate folks to follow them" (90).[9]

Sidney's sharp distinction between factual truth and poetic truth, and his subsequent dismissal of the former as inferior to the latter in its moral efficacy, represent one of the two defenses of poetic fiction available to Jonson and his contemporaries. Indeed, if fiction is inseparably associated with falsehood, the poet has two alternatives to free himself from the charge of lying. Sidney's justification is one. The other course is by way of insisting that what is called fiction is no fiction at all, but a true report of things as they are. As we have seen, Jonson uses both justifications, sometimes juxtaposing them. By using both, he professes simultaneous allegiance to history and poetry, or to the truth of fact and the moral utility of fiction. In other words, he has it both ways: although he normally stresses the truth of his praise, he will nevertheless use the justification that fiction is morally useful whenever the problem of overpraise cannot be overlooked.

The genre of epideictic poetry itself, which typically thrives on the interaction between fact and fiction, necessitates such a dual allegiance. Literary theorists since Plato, as O. B. Hardison notes, emphasized the genre's reliance on history. They agreed with Menander and the author of the *Rhetorica ad Herennium* that since epideictic poetry is about actual events or actual persons it should be based on historical facts, such as a person's nature, fortune, and character. But the historical facts must be contained in a form of praise; facts must be shaped into a fictive form. And the evolution of Renaissance epideictics, which Jonson's poetry embodies and inevitably modifies, can be traced along the course it took to break away from the "straight-jacket" (in Hardison's word) of factual truth as the basis of poetry and to readmit fiction as a legitimate element of poetry.[10]

There are of course practical reasons for the epideictic poet to seek a harmony between fact and fiction. The common charge leveled against the epideictic poet is that his praise is flattery. When the poet writes about contemporary events and living people, he is patently vulnerable to the charge of lying, fawning eloquence, mercenary flattery, and servility. The same poetic fiction that the epideictic poet uses as a means of instruction and admonishment may be received by the reader as a piece of flattery or a guise of extortion. Jonson's own case abundantly tells us what penalties an epideictic poet has to pay. With all his protestations of integrity, he was not able to free himself from the charge of mercenary motives in his epideictic composition. In 1680, writing of Jonson's success in the "trade" of versing, Isaac Walton cast a dark glance at Jonson's probity as a praiser and satirist. He reports that Jonson received "100^{li} a yeare from the king, also a pention from the Cittie, and the like from many of the nobilitie, and som of the gentry. W^{c}h was well pay'd for love or fere of his raling in verse, or prose, or boeth" (*H&S* 1:181). Penalties came from another direction as well. The topical allusions included in epideictic poems could all too easily irritate the "Jacobethan" court's touchy sensitivity as buried criticism. Perhaps no one would have known the danger better than Jonson, who had more than once landed in prison on charges of libel.[11]

The epideictic poet's task to turn history into poetry, then, requires a skillful balancing between fact and fiction. The person who sets out to write on contemporary events and living persons needs must learn what facts would appropriately be included and what should be suppressed. In the Renaissance, as the age's numerous poems of fulsome praise amply testify, the balance more often than not tilts to fiction, perhaps for the obvious reason that patterns of virtue are usually hard to find in real life. The Renaissance epideictic poet had every reason to emphasize the truth and moral value of fiction and in the same breath to insist on the integrity of his praise.

How to adhere to facts in praising, which includes by nature and of necessity a certain amount of idealization, and how to reconcile the conflicting demands of fact and fiction in the poems themsleves, are the problems the epideictic poet has to deal with. O. B. Hardison notes that one of the solutions to the epideictic poet's problems was the theory of *pictura*, "the poetic form of exemplary narrative": "The two concepts of historical narrative and example of virtue or vice meet in *pictura*. They are present because *pictura* has the two epideictic functions of imitating an individual and creating a pattern that will arouse emulation or abhorrence."[12] Making patterns of vice and virtue out of a veritable chaos of already constituted events, as Hardison rightly observes, inevitably involves a process of idealization. The epideictic poet creates his *pictura* by stressing some events and withholding others, or by altering some and inventing others.

Whatever Jonson's protestations about his honesty in praising, the basic method of his epideictic poetry is that of *pictura* with all its idealizing tendencies. Through *pictura* Jonson strives to mediate between a factual representation of his subject—portraying the very person—and a more idealized or ennobled representation. But the idealizing impulse is by far the stronger of the two. And the attempt to achieve a factual representation becomes in practice an attempt to maintain an impression of factual truth.[13]

The playfully hyperbolic praise of the Penshurst estate illustrates the method Jonson uses to create an ideal picture out of real things without entirely taking leave of factual truth. The following lines show an obvious tendency toward idealization (*Forest* 2, "To Penshurst"):

> The painted partrich lyes in every field,
>   And, for thy messe, is willing to be kill'd.
> And if the high-swolne *Medway* faile thy dish,
>   Thou hast thy ponds, that pay thee tribute fish,
> Fat, aged carps, that runne into thy net.
>   And pikes, now weary their owne kind to eat,
> As loth, the second draught, or cast to stay,
>   Officiously, at first, themselves betray.
> Bright eeles, that emulate them, and leape on land
>   Before the fisher, or into his hand.   (29–38)

Raymond Williams has complained that the base-stuff of this rarified picture is the gore and grease that stocks the real-life dining table.[14] One does not have to agree with him to say that the "painted" partridge willing to be killed and the "officious" fish leaping into the fisher's hand are not quite like such game in real life. By describing them as willing to perform their offices in the natural order as food for men, Jonson turns the real partridge around Penshurst and the real fish in Medway into emblems of the concord between men and nature, and the real Penshurst estate into a *pictura* of ideal society.

But Jonson insists on the factual basis of this idealized picture.[15] As the fish leap from the particular river Medway, this ideal natural order is localized: it has the name of Penshurst. It calls the reader's attention to its identity as Penshurst, a particular place situated in a particular region and inhabited by particular people. Moreover, it is something that Jonson himself can directly experience. With men and natural beings heightened and idealized to a mythic dimension, there appears in the poem Jonson's corpulent self, fraught with memories of the harsh reality beyond his ideal Penshurst. Jonson praises Penshurst

> Where comes no guest, but is allow'd to eate,
>   Without his feare, and of thy lords own meate:
> Where the same beere, and bread, and self-same wine,
>   That is his Lordships, shall be also mine.
> And I not faine to sit (as some, this day,
>   At great mens tables) and yet dine away.
> Here no men tells my cups; nor, standing by,
>   A waiter, doth my gluttony envy:
> But gives me what I call, and lets me eate.   (61–69)

By representing himself as a direct beneficiary of the ideal natural order at Penshurst, Jonson not only praises the estate but gives his praise the sanction of an observed and experienced fact.

In thus idealizing Penshurst, Jonson conveys an impression of factuality and tries to communicate conviction by presenting the virtue of Penshurst as his personal experience. This dual commitment to fact and fiction is responsible, I think, for the specificity of his praise, which Barbara K. Lewalski identifies as Jonson's contribution to the evolution of the poetry-of-praise tradition in England. In *Donne's "Anniversaries" and the Poetry of Praise,* she maintains that "Ben Jonson elevated to new poetic heights this conception of praise as involving a stance of forthright, judicious honesty and precise definition of the topic of virtue in terms of specific qualities and actions"; his poetry signals the trend "toward more orderly structure and more analytic development in the poem of compliment."[16] She cites as an example the epigram "To Thomas Lord Chancelor [Egerton]" (*Epigrammes* 74):

> Whil'st thy weigh'd judgements, EGERTON, I heare,
>   And know thee, then, a judge, not of one yeare;
> Whil'st I behold thee live with purest hands;
>   That no affection in thy voyce commands;
> That still th'art present to the better cause;
>   And no lesse wise, than skillful in the lawes;
> Whil'st thou art certaine to thy words, once gone,
>   As is thy conscience, which is alwayes one:
> The Virgin, long-since fled from earth, I see,
>   T[o] our times return'd, hath made her heaven in thee.

The poem does indeed define "the topic of virtue in terms of specific qualities and actions" of the person praised. Most appropriately for praise of a Lord Chancellor, it concentrates on Egerton's integrity and conscientiousness.

So far Lewalski's formulation of Jonson's method in praise accurately describes the poem. But, perhaps because her main interest in this book is in Donne's epideictic method, she leaves it unremarked that the final effect of Jonson's specificity in praising an actual person is not a realistic description of the person but a highly idealized representation. Indeed, from associating a person with a specific moral quality it is only a short distance to representing the person as an embodiment of that specific moral quality. In that sense, Jonson's method of setting "the topic of virtue in terms of specific qualities" is more similar to than different from what Lewalski describes as Donne's "symbolic mode" in *Anniversaries,* a mode of idealization that turns an actual person into an "incarnation of virtue, or goodness, or divinity."[17]

Jonson's Egerton in this poem is not the historical Egerton but an ideal judge created out of that historical judge. Egerton embodies in himself all the attributes of this ideal: impartiality in judgment, wisdom and skill in the laws, and integrity in speech. And by the end of the poem, when Jonson identifies Egerton with Astraea, the goddess of law and justice, Egerton the particular judge is made into the universal idea of justice, a virtual as well as virtuous personification. Here Jonson reverses the usual procedure for creating a personification: instead of fleshing out a preconceived moral concept, he first associates an actual person with a moral ideal and then permeates that person with specific attributes of that ideal till he becomes the ideal itself. This process of creating an ideal actual is literally the action of the poem "On Lucy Countesse of Bedford" (*Epigrammes* 76), another of Lewalski's examples. The poem tells its own story:

> This morning, timely rapt with holy fire,
>   I thought to forme unto my zealous *Muse,*
> What kinde of creature I could most desire,
>   To honour, serve, and love; as *Poets* use.
> I meant to make her faire, and free, and wise,
>   Of greatest bloud, and yet more good then great;
> I meant the day-starre should not brighter rise,
>   Nor lend like influence from his lucent seat.
> I meant shee should be curteous, facile, sweet,
>   Hating that solemne vice of greatnesse, pride;
> I meant each softest vertue, there should meet,
>   Fit in that softer bosome to reside.
> Only a learned, and a manly soule
>   I propos'd her; that should, with even powers,
> The rock, the spindle, and the sheeres controule
>   Of destinie, and spin her owne free houres.
> Such when I meant to faine, and wish'd to see,
>   My *Muse* bad, *Bedford* write, and that was shee.

Endowed with moral qualities, specified and catalogued, the woman Lucy Bedford becomes an embodiment of perfect womanhood. The actual is turned into an ideal but still retains the name Lucy Bedford. If there is a gap between the actual and the ideal, it can be seen only by those who know the woman praised and idealized by Jonson.

Indeed, the major rhetorical device used in these two epigrams, as in "To Penshurst," is hyperbole, but it is a hyperbole constructed to conceal its own presence. In "To Penshurst," this device undercuts the process of idealization, even while activating it, because the trope operates precisely upon the transparent difference between fact and its exaggeration. The idealizing tendency, far from seeming to disappear, is so exaggerated that the reader is made aware of its presence. And when it is recognized by the reader as such, as it certainly is in the passage on the officious fish and partridge, it inevitably becomes self-referential, declaring the fundamental fictiveness of the picture it creates. But in the epigram to Egerton, the gap between the person and the moral quality personified by the person, far from being laid bare, is made to disappear. The personification of justice is simply presented as Egerton, and the identity of Egerton the historical figure is insisted on. "Egerton" is called into the text of the poem itself, and his existence is attested by the poet, who insists that he knows Egerton, the then and now judge, and by the testimony of his highest senses: "Whil'st . . . I heare / And know thee . . . Whil'st I behold thee . . . I see . . . [the Virgin] in thee."

Hyperbole in this epigram to Egerton works like what J. B. Leishman calls Shakespeare's "un-Platonic hyperbole." In Jonson's idealized picture of Egerton, as in Shakespeare's idealized image of his fair friend, the distinction between actual and ideal no longer remains. Like Shakespeare's friend, Jonson's Egerton is presented not as a reminder of a Platonic idea but as "*the archetype, pattern, idea, or ideal*" itself.[18] But Jonson's insistence on the factuality of his hyperbolical praise should alert us to the basic difference between Jonson and Shakespeare in their epideictic use of hyperbole. Shakespeare, Leishman observes, uses "un-Platonic hyperbole" not as a rhetorical device but as the only possible expression of what his friend means to him. If he is right, and I think he is, the gap between fact and its hyperbolical representation would become a problem for the poet only when the hyperbole fails to convey what he has to express. Where the expressive power of the hyperbole is the issue, its factual truth need not be insisted on. That Jonson insists on the factual truth of his hyperboles suggests that he is dealing with a problem different from what might have been Shakespeare's.[19] His is not how to represent an ideal actual person that he believes to exist, but how to convince the reader of the existence of that ideal actual person. He has to use hyperbole without revealing its idealizing tendency actively at work.

In Jonson's double process of idealizing and creating an impression of factual truth, the poet—through what he says he has experienced—plays a crucial role. Neither the historical fact that "To Penshurst" was composed when Sir Robert Sidney was undergoing one of his worst financial embarrassments and when English rural society as a whole was experiencing structural changes, nor the fact that to some of his contemporaries Egerton, the Viscount Brackley, was "Break-law," has made its way into the poems to render them factually true.[20] It is only the testimony of the poet that gives a name and locality to what would otherwise be an imaginative construct: Jonson's Penshurst is a picture of an ideal society but is presented as an actual place, just as his Egerton is an embodiment of justice without ceasing to be called Egerton. This impression of factual truth created by the articulate presence of the poet in the poem points to another major strategy Jonson uses to reconcile fact and fiction in his poems of praise. In his praise of Robert,

Earl of Salisbury (*Epigrammes* 63), Jonson diverts the reader's attention from the idealizing process. He asks:

> Who can consider thy right courses run,
>> With what thy vertue on the times hath won,
> And not thy fortune; who can cleerely see
>> The judgment of the king so shine in thee;
> And that thou seek'st reward of thy each act,
>> Not from the publike voyce, but private fact;
> Who can behold all envie so declin'd
>> By constant suffering of thy equall mind;
> And can to these be silent, *Salisburie,*
>> Without his, thine, and all times injurie?
> Curst be his *Muse,* that could lye dumbe, or hid
>> To so true worth, though thou thy selfe forbid.

As Richard C. Newton observes, in the rhetorical question the poet rejects Salisbury's outer reality ("fortune" and "publike voyce"), but emphasizes his inner reality ("vertue" and "private fact"), as the basis of his praise.[21] But the poet does not explain what Salisbury's "vertue" and "private fact" really are. In the concluding couplet he merely asserts that his praise is freely given in spite of the objection of the person praised, and given for the sake of truth. In this praise Salisbury's virtue is not reproduced but indicated: *res gesta* gives way to the voice of praise. He praises Salisbury not by describing his virtue but by claiming his knowledge of it, not by emphasizing desert but by announcing his decision to praise it. The center of the poem's attention becomes the praiser as much as the person praised, and the whole poem is made into a commentary on the act of praising as much as an act of praise.

This strategy of diverting the reader's attention from the idealizing process by denying the need to idealize and by shifting the focus of the poem from the person praised to the person(a) praising has its corollary in the most significant of the modifications Jonson has brought to the traditional genre of epideictic poetry, the identification of the praised and the praiser, one of the "paths" that Jonson meant unto the praise of Shakespeare. In "To the Memory of My Beloved the Author Mr. William Shakespeare and What He Left Us" (*Ungathered Verse* 26), Jonson invests Shakespeare with the qualities he most prizes in an artist and in himself; he gives "art" to a poet whose lack of art he censures elsewhere: "Yet must I not give Nature all: Thy Art, / My gentle *Shakespeare,* must enjoy a part" (55–56).[22]

4

Jonson's Meta-Masques and the Poet King

Some Elizabethan and Jacobean masque writers regard the masque's relationship to the world of facts as tenuous. Francis Bacon curtly dismisses court masques as mere princely recreations: they are "but toys, to come amongst such serious observations." For Samuel Daniel, they are not only entertainments but also an idealization of the court, their purpose being to display royal power and magnificence. In his preface to *The Vision of Twelve Goddesses* (1603–4), he characterizes his task as being to contribute to state and greatness, to make, as he puts it, a "hieroglyphic of empire and dominion." The intent of his masque, appropriately, is not to represent the actual King James and his lords but to idealize them: it is "only to present the figures of those blessings, with the wish of their increase and continuance, which this mighty kingdom now enjoys by the benefit of his most gracious Majesty, by whom we have this glory of peace, with the accession of so great state and power." Where only pleasure and propaganda are the concern, the question of factuality is simply irrelevant.[1]

Jonson differs from both Bacon and Daniel in that he acknowledges the factual origin of this most idealized, and most political, of all literary genres. Even when he argues for the necessity of transcending the immediate circumstances of particular occasions, his impulse toward fact compels him to suggest that the fiction of masques should be conveyed through the language that the facts of specific occasions constitute: "though their [masques's] *voice* be taught to sound to present occasions, their *sense,* or doth, or should always lay hold on more remov'd *mysteries*" (preface to *Hymenaei*, 1606). Thus the "more remov'd *mysteries*" of *Hymenaei*—the new union of England and Scotland, the union of King James and his kingdom, or the cosmic union wrought by the power of love—are articulated through the *"voice"* of the specific marriage of the Earl of Essex and Frances Howard.[2]

George Chapman, whom Jonson pronounced to be the most able masque writer next to himself, in the preface to his *Masque of the Middle Temple and Lincoln's Inn* (1613) expresses the same idea, but with a clearer stress on the factual basis of the masque:

I am forced to affirm this: that as there is no poem nor oration so general, but hath his one particular proposition; nor no river so extravagantly ample, but hath his never-so-narrow fountain, worthy to be named; so all these courtly and honouring inventions (having poesy and oration in them, and a fountain to be expressed, from whence their rivers flow) should expressively arise out of the places and persons for and by whom they are presented; without which limits they are luxurious and vain.[3]

Chapman's assertion that even an admittedly fictional construct like the masque should be based on and framed by fact can serve us as a bridge between Jonson's suggestion in the preface to *Hymenaei* and his definition of the genre as a criticism of life in the preface to *Love's Triumph Through Callipolis* (1631). At the end of his career as a masque writer, Jonson describes his masques as as fully committed to representation of reality as any other serious literary form: they "either have bene, or ought to be the mirrors of mans life, whose ends, for the excellence of their exhibitors (as being the donatives of, great Princes, to their people) ought always to carry a mixture of profit, with them, no lesse then delight" (*H&S* 7:735.4–7). Jonson, quite obviously, considers his masques as a part of his epideictic poetry. His redefinition of the masque brings into high relief the problematic relationship of epideictic genres to the world of particular facts: the masque purports to refashion the factual world by representing it; it represents it by idealizing it; and it defies it while celebrating it. The genre binds the masque writer in a double obligation to the actual and ideal worlds, presenting him with a series of ethical, philosophical, and technical problems: How is it possible for one to be still in the world of facts, while pursuing one's impulse toward the ideal version of that world? How is it possible to contain factual reality in a statement about the ideal world? How is it possible to maintain the illusion of factuality while stripping the factual world of its particularity? On the solution to these problems hangs Jonson's self-imposed mission to make the genre a serious literary form that always carries "a mixture of profit, with them, no lesse then delight."

The masque as Jonson conceives it, then, presents the masque writer with the epideictic poet's problem. Leah Sinanoglou Marcus's recent articles on *Plea-*

sure Reconciled to Virtue, The Vision of Delight, Christmas His Masque,
and *The Golden Age Restored,* and Dale B. J. Randall's book on *Gypsies
Metamorphosed* have shown that Jonson indeed mixed fact with fiction in
his masques.[4] His hyperbolical praise of the king contains commentaries on
sensitive contemporary issues, advice to the king, or sometimes genial satire
against favorites and courtiers. High topicality, however, is not the only
consequence of his attempt to fuse fact and fiction in his masques. The
attempt also results in the creation of the meta-masque, a radical modification of the traditional court masque. The textual strategies he uses in his
poems of praise in order to achieve an appearance of factuality point to an
increasing self-consciousness in his work as a whole. As we saw in the
previous chapter, the focus of the poem of praise is shifted from the praised to
the praiser, and from the praise to the act of praising itself. Typical Jonsonian
masques show the same tendency to reflect on the poet and his fictionalizing.
Jonson turns the genre into a probing examination of its nature as fiction and
creates as a result a masque that can better serve the initial and ultimate
impulse of the genre to praise and educate the prince and his court.

The masque is an epideictic medium very different from nondramatic
epideictic poetry. In a sense, the appearance of factuality, which Jonson
strives to achieve through a series of textual strategies in his epigrams of
praise, is generically ensured in the masque by its power to visualize fiction.[5]
Indeed the persuasive power of the masque as an epideictic form depends in
large part on its exploitation of theatrical illusions. Its praise is made appre-
hensible: abstract moral qualities are physically embodied by the very persons to whom they are attributed. Details of surface—dazzling ornaments,
costumes, and illusionist scenery used almost exclusively for masques—
conspire to actualize the ideals that the masque tries to propagate. Gods and
goddesses, mythical queens, and fairy kings and knights visit the court in
person and mingle with actual courtiers, absorbing the actual into the ideal
world of the masque.

The course Jonson has taken in his striving to introduce fact into the fiction
of the masque has largely been determined by his suspicion of fiction and the
disguise that makes fiction seem real. His chief device for achieving a fusion
of fact and fiction in the masque is to shatter rather than to foster theatrical
illusions. His impatience with the costly ritual of making fiction seem real is
expressed most controversially in his attacks on Inigo Jones and the theatrical illusions his spectacle aims at creating.[6] In the preface to *Hymenaei,* now
a *locus classicus* in the brief life story of the masque genre, Jonson relegates
Jones's spectacle to the realm of bodily things, eminently perishable and thus
deceptive: spectacle is the body, while poetry is the soul, of the masque, the
one "but momentary and merely taking, the other impressing and lasting." In
"An Expostulation with Inigo Jones" (*Ungathered Verse* 34), he makes it

clear that what he resents about the architect's spectacle is its concentration on the externals, its tendency to visualize even the "more remov'd *mysteries*" of the masque, leaving no room for his poetry:

> O Showes! Showes! Mighty Showes!
> The Eloquence of Masques! What need of prose
> Or Verse, or Sense t'express Immortall you?
> You are the Spectacles of State! 'Tis true
> Court Hieroglyphicks! and all Artes affoord
> In the mere perspective of an inch board!
> You aske noe more then certeine politique eyes,
> Eyes that can pierce into the Mysteries
> Of many Colours! read them! and reveal
> Mythology there painted on slit deale!
> Oh, to make Boardes to speake! There is a taske
> Painting and Carpentry are the Soul of Masque.   (39–50)

Jonson's distrust of what occupies the eye to the exclusion of the mind, vehemently expressed in these lines, has much to do with his deep-seated suspicion of shows of things, a suspicion that characterizes his work as a whole. In fact, he seems to have viewed the world as a dual structure of appearance and reality. Throughout his work, the conflict between body and soul, appearance and reality, is as pervasive as it is multifarious in its forms: the word that cannot contain the thing, the name that cannot match the identity, the mask that hides the face, and the gorgeous dress that gilds over the rotten body underneath are his emblems for the original fissure between body and soul, the "shame, and scorne" that he has to share with all children of Adam in his cold exile from heaven (*Forest* 15, "To Heaven"). Tailors' creatures stalk in the world of his satiric epigrams, whose air convulses with the stench of powdering, painting, and simpering dames, while rituals of uncasing such soulless cases bring many Volpones and Faces to their comedies' ends.

The appearance of factuality that the masque's fiction acquires with the aid of theatrical illusions is transitory as well as lacking in substance, like shadows of shadows, dreams of dreams. Stuart masque writers' musings on the genre's evanescence are a warning against such appearance of factuality as much as a subdued voice of disenchantment at the fleeting visions of delight. Daniel's song in *Tethys' Festival* (1610) is an example as good as any:[7]

> Are they shadowes that we see?
> And can shadowes pleasure give?
>   Pleasure onely shadowes bee
>   Cast by bodies we conceive,

> And are made the thinges we deeme,
> In those figures which they seeme.
> But these pleasures vanish fast,
> Which by shadowes are exprest
> > Pleasures are not, if they last,
> > In their passing, is their best
> > Glory is most bright and gay
> > In a flash, and so away.
> Feed apace then greedy eyes
> On the wonder you behold.
> > Take it sodaine as it flies
> > Though you take it not to hold:
> > When your eyes have done their part,
> > Thought must length it in the hart.   (341–58)

Delicately poised as they are, these lines betray Daniel's disturbing insight into the insubstantiality of the masque's vision—"shadowes" that the imagination figures forth—which eventually led him away from fabricating poetic fiction to recording facts.

The masque's vision is not just impermanent; it can also be morally dangerous. The fiction actualized through theatrical illusions not only seems fact but sometimes becomes fact. Thus Charles I, as C. V. Wedgwood and other historians point out, defied the tumultous reality outside the court, shutting himself up in a self-celebrating vision of permanence and transcendence that the Caroline court masques so abundantly provided. The world of ideal fiction, for all practical purposes, becomes the only substantial world, while the world of fact fades into a nightmarish, but ultimately insubstantial, pageant.[8]

Writing two centuries later, Percy Bysshe Shelley translated into his own terms the ambiguous effects of the masque's vision on both the audience and the masquers. He begins his unfinished tragedy *Charles the First* with dramatizing two different responses to the fiction that James Shirley's masque *Triumph of Peace* created for the king in 1634.[9] The older citizens denounce as sinister the masque's inversion of fact and fiction. First Citizen asks,

> What thinkest thou of this quaint masque which turns,
> Like morning from the shadow of the night,
> The night to day, and London to a place
> Of peace and joy?

Second Citizen quickly supplies the oracular half line:

> And Hell to Heaven.   (1.1.2–5)

But A Youth's perception is something different:

'tis like the bright procession
Of skiey visions in a solemn dream
From which men wake as from a Paradise,
And draw new strength to tread the thorns of life. (1.1.17–20)

For Shelley the radical difference between fact and fiction is not the "vanity" (1.1.6) of Narcissuses, as it was for his elders, but a source of the strength that makes "the thorns of life" more bearable. As David Norbrook rightly points out, Shelley's dramatization captures the complex relationship between art and reality. The masque's vision could become an anodyne to alleviate for a while the pain and demand of pressing reality; but its impulse to go beyond the brute facts of life—to search "May flowers" "which bloom so rarely in this barren world" of quotidian experiences (as A Youth puts it in line 24)—could become a spur to the will to actualize the vision in real life.[10] The masque can be a powerful instrument for a radical reformation of the social reality. And the two possibilities—seduction into moral blindness, and education toward radical reformation—reside in the same medium and in a continuum.

Jonson, who shares Shelley's didactic impulse, responds to the masque's vision in a similar way. He tries to minimize the danger of the vision by exposing its artificiality. The real world introduced into the masque in order to shatter its illusion of factuality in turn substantiates its idealistic vision. Jonson vindicates the power of true poetry to reform the world by overcoming the seductive power of poetic fiction now made more dangerous with the aid of theatrical illusion. This response to the masque's vision informs the structure of a typical Jonsonian meta-masque: it shatters the appearance of factuality that the masque's fiction acquires through theatrical illusion, and it does this in order to vindicate the true transforming power of poetic fiction.

The Jonsonian masque is, in more ways than one, a crystallization of Jonson's dualistic vision of the world and the function of poetry in it. What might be called anti-illusionism, stemming from his suspicion of appearance, colors his conception of the masque. To understand this, one must examine how he uses the masque in *Cynthia's Revels* (1600). Written five years earlier than his first masque, *The Masque of Blackness* (1605), the play is an anatomy of the masque, revealing not only its function and power but its dangerous tendency to disguise reality in a better-seeming cloak.[11] Jonson dislocates and rearranges the conventions of the masque to satisfy his impulse toward fact. The concluding masque of the play has all the necessary ingredients of a conventional masque: a procession of allegorical personages, representing eight courtly virtues, is led by truchmen to the presiding sovereign. But what is surprising is that the device of the masque hinges on the fact that these figures are not virtues but vices masquerading in the guise of virtues. There opens a wide gap between their spiritual reality and their outward appearance, the latter only emphasizing the severe deficiency of the former. The masque threatens to become a ceremony of perpetuating self-deception, not only for the false courtiers but, more frighteningly, for Cynthia herself, whose veiled vision cannot yet penetrate the deceptive outward forms to distinguish mask from face. The masque presented as a celebration of Cynthia is on the verge of becoming a profanation of her as well as a self-congratulation of the false courtiers. This is a ruthless unmasking of the conventions of the masque to show that its concentration on appearance is profoundly deceptive.

The conventional idea of the masque as a celebration of the idealized picture of the court is turned into a satire of the court that cannot live up to that ideal. The disjunction between the conventional use of the masque and Crites' use of the masque in this play is a measure of the distance the court has traveled from its ideal image as a "bountifull, and brave spring" that "water-est all the noble plants of this Iland" to the fatal "Spring of selfe-Love." The masque, which should mirror the reality of the court, has become a false glass that encourages the court's self-deceiving admiration of its own image, beau-tified not by "a mind, shining through any sute, which needes no false light either of riches, or honors to helpe it" but by "pould'ring, perfuming, and every day smelling of the tailor" (Dedicatory Epistle to the Court, *Cynthia's Revels*).

The masque's concentration on appearance is a natural corollary to the court's concentration on the superficial. It is not surprising, then, that Arete and Crites should devise a presentation of a masque as a measure for pu-rification. The unmasking of the masque convention by shattering its ap-pearance of truth is in a very real sense an unmasking of the court. Crites turns the masque, which is normally a ritual of celebration of virtues, into a ritual of exposing vices.[12] But, significantly, by shattering the appearance of virtue, he also purges his masque of its characteristic unconventionality. The procession of false courtiers, now exposed and penitent, in their pilgrimage toward Niobe the weeping stone, is a masque celebrating poetry's potent power to reform the vicious into the virtuous, which, as Crites takes pains to make clear, emanates from Cynthia, the sister of Phoebus. Their palinode becomes, by Crites' double twist of masque conventions, a true eulogy of Cynthia and the power of poetry.

Crites' success as a reformer lies precisely in his successful attempt to defeat the deceiving vision of the masque. His exposing of the false courtiers questions the legitimacy of theatrical maneuvers to make fiction seem fact, but that radical questioning is in turn used to strengthen his defense of poetry as educative. It is clear in Crites' masque that Jonson is conscious of the ambiguous nature of fiction. It can educate the audience by presenting them with embodiments of ideals. It can reform the masquers acting as the embodiments of the ideals, as Beaurline points out, by compelling them to become what they are represented to be.[13] But it can also feed and water the passion of self-love, the admiration of one's own image reflected in the beautiful fiction of the masque. The masque can be a trap of self delusion for those who cannot see their true faces. It can be fatally seductive, a fact amply demonstrated by what became of the player-king, Charles I, who held the fictional world of the masque as a plea against the overwhelming tide of rebellion.

Crites' masque is Jonson's probing examination of the nature of the masque and its idealized fiction. In this masque the morally dangerous power of praise is counteracted by the satiric elements brought into that fiction, which in turn set the masque's reforming power in motion. The exposing of the fissure between mask and face prepares the way to its healing in the final scene of the masque. The masque as a whole becomes a pilgrimage toward the restoration of the unity between body and soul, mask and face. And this compound of satire and eulogy—Crites' strategic use of satire in aid of eulogy—anticipates the structural division of a characteristic Jonsonian masque into the satiric and realistic antimasque and the eulogistic and idealistic main masque.

Crites not only converts the false into true courtiers but also changes an exposing into a healing ritual. His exposing is an antimasque in its nascent form, but it also contains the seed of the main masque. Jonson's later masques typically divide these elements into two distinct structural units: the antimasque serves as an outlet for the expression of reality suppressed and transformed into the vision that the main masque offers. And this transition from exposing to healing also marks the movement toward the final vindication of the reforming power of poetry, which the disruption of theatrical illusion only facilitates.

Jonson's later masques show indications of increasing self-consciousness of the artificiality of the masque's vision and the masquing occasion. The antimasques, as a rule, become occasions for theorizing before the audience on the craft of masque making. They are masques on masques. This tendency is first displayed in its full force in *Love Restored*, performed at court on Twelfth Night, 1612.[14] Its ostensible theme—restoring Love's reign usurped by Plutus the Mammon—is familiar enough, but its real concern is nothing less than the nature of the masque genre itself. It begins with a masquerado (who proves to be a character named Masquerado) announcing that the performance has been canceled. Something has gone amiss backstage, he says, and

In troth, Ladies, I pittie you all. You are here in expectation of a device to night, and I am afraid you can doe little else but expect it. Though I dare not shew my face, I can speake truth, under a vizard. Good faith, an 't please your Majestie, Your Masquers are all at a stand; I cannot thinke your Majesty will see any shew to night, at least worth your patience. (1–9)

With this announcement, he steps out of the masque into the world outside of it, obliterating at once the boundary between fact and fiction, audience and performer. The distinction between the world of fact and the world of fiction is further blurred in the rest of his apology, where he discloses the process of masque making.

Some two houres since, we were in that forwardnesse, our dances learn'd, our masquing attire on and attired. A prettie fine speech was taken up o'the Poet too, which if hee never be paid for, now, it's no matter; His wit costs him nothing. Unless wee should come in like a Morrice-dance, and whistle our ballat our selves, I know not what we should doe: we ha' no other Musician to play our tunes, but the wild musique here, and the rogue play-boy that acts Cupid is got so hoarse, your majestie cannot heare him, halfe the bredth o'your chayre. (9–18)

Masquerado's one-man show asserts its factuality by exposing the artificiality of the masque, of which it is a part. For him the masque is no different from any other theatrical production. Its idealistic vision, like any other, is to be produced by the art of script writers, musicians, stage designers, and actors: if "the rogue play-boy that acts Cupid is got so hoarse," well, then, the masque cannot be. Gods never descend from heaven without the aid of stagecraft.

This initial confusion of fact and fiction emerges as the controlling device of the masque. Fiction is repeatedly declared to be fact and then exposed as fiction. Masquerado's vizarded "truth" swiftly meets a challenge in Plutus, disguised as Cupid. He bursts into the hall to interrupt Masquerado's show that cancels the show, eliciting from him a bewildered response: "Ha'you recovered your voice, to rail at me?" (27). But Masquerado (and the audience with him) is mistaken in his assumption that Plutus is a "play-boy"; for the disguised Cupid claims that he is "neither player, nor masquer; but the god himselfe, whose deitie is here profan'd" (28–29). Having disclaimed the fictionality of his being, he takes the audience by surprise, leading them into a deeper confusion of fact and fiction. He came here, he says, not to put on a show but to abolish the institution of masquing itself, which is for him an unthrifty vanity: "I tell thee, I will have no more masquing; I will not buy a false, and fleeting delight so deare. The merry madnesse of one houer shall not cost me the repentance of an age" (34–36).[15] But, Plutus's "facts" are in turn proved to be factitious, as Robin Goodfellow unmasks "that Imposter

PLUTUS, the god of *money,* who ha's stolne LOVE'S ensignes; and in his belied figure reignes ⟨i'⟩ the world, making friendships, contracts, marriages, and almost religion; begetting, breeding and holding the neerest respects of mankind; and usurping all those offices in this Age of gold, which LOVE himselfe perform'd in the golden age" (173–79).

The ground of the masque's fiction is shifting: the worlds of fact and fiction become increasingly indistinguishable from each other. The three characters—Masquerado, Plutus, and Robin Goodfellow—assert and partly prove their reality by reexamining the nature and practice of masquings and court entertainments. Their views, which place the genre firmly in the context of social and economic realities, are in turn a measure of their own reality. Masquerado's emphasis on the artificiality of the genre is replaced by Plutus's denunciation: "Away, idle spirit; and thou, the idle cause of his adventring hither, vanish with him. 'Tis thou, that art not only the sower of vanities, in these high places, but the call of all other light follies to fall, and feed on them. I will endure thy prodigalitie, nor riots no more; they are the ruine of states. Nor shall the tyrannie of these nights, hereafter impose a necessitie upon me, of entertaining thee. Let'hem embrace more frugall pastimes" (144–51). Plutus's outrage at the extravagance of court entertainment introduces to the ideal world of the masque a *memento mori,* an uncomfortable reminder of the ideal world's utter dependence upon the material world: without Plutus and his money, that is, his materialism, the masque cannot proceed. The ideal world is all but engulfed by the material world in Robin Goodfellow's account of the obstacles he has surmounted in order to gain entry to the masquing hall. His realistic descriptions of those who have gathered around the court for the masquing occasion show the masque to be not so much a celebration of pale ideals as a catalyst in the frantically boiling fleshpot of the world. The women whom masquing occasions attract, for example, are radically different from the goddesses of masques: "Mary before I could procure my properties, alarum came, that some o' the whim-len's ⟨had⟩ had too much; and one shew'd how fruitfully they had watered his head, as hee stood under the grices; and another came out complaining of a cataract, shot into his eyes, by a planet, as hee was starre-gazing" (110–15).

The world of reality closes in on the world of the masque with smothering intensity. But these characters' extreme realism is countered by the official view of the masque expounded in the main masque: it is a celebration of the king's virtue, whose "powerful beames of light and heat" can thaw the "icie fetters, and scatter the darknesse that obscures" Love (195–97). The one who most devastatingly exposes the masque's evil effect, Robin Goodfellow, is also the harbinger of Love, the presiding spirit of the masque. He is percipient enough to discern the poverty of Plutus's spirit and his niggardly "facts," which reduce the genre to a mere pastime. By exposing Plutus, he is able to redirect the audience's attention to the original spirit of the masque and thus restore the reign of Love. The fiction of the main masque finally triumphs over the reality introduced in the antimasque.

The idealization of the king derives much of its impact from its triumph over the pervasive realism. Robin Goodfellow praises the king for his virtue, which frees the true masque from the fetters of real life; for the problems of the masque represented by Masquerado, Plutus, and Robin Goodfellow disappear in the final epiphany of Love. *Love Restored* turns out to be a characteristically Jonsonian debate between fact and fiction, and its questions about the masque's social function turn out to be a commentary on the perennial problem of poetry's relationship to the world of facts.

The tendency of Jonson's later masques to become meta-masques is significant for the masque genre as a praise of the king. The writer of a meta-masque must find a way to relate the king to the craft of masque making in order to turn an examination of the problems of the genre into a praise of him. In *Love Restored*, Jonson praises the king for his power to resolve the problems of the genre: the king is not only the sponsor of the masque but also its creator, because he alone can free the world of ideals from the tyranny of facts. In his meta-masques after *Love Restored*, notably in *Mercury Vindicated from the Alchemists at Court* (1616), *The Golden Age Restored* (1616), *News from the New World* (1620), *The Masque of Augurs* (1622), and *Time Vindicated to Himself and to His Honors* (1623), Jonson regularly invests the king with the creative power of the Sidneian poet to deliver a golden world from the brazen world of facts, thus converting the king into an archetypal poet, and a celebration of the king into a vindication of poetry.

In *Love Restored*, the transformation of the king into an archetypal poet is prefigured in the sudden change of Robin Goodfellow the satiric commentator into a praiser. In a way, the meta-masque as a whole is organized around the progression of the satirist into a panegyrist. The clear vision of the satirist, which has enabled him to see and expose the true shapes of things behind their shows, also enables him to see and praise the workings of the king's creative, transforming power. This organizing principle, if in an embryonic form, is already at work in Jonson's early masques, which conform more closely to the conventions of the genre than do his later ones. It is discernible in *The Masque of Blackness* (1605), his first masque. Leading a procession of Æthiopes into the masquing hall, Niger, their harassed father, complains about the "brainsick" fable makers:

> Yet, since the fabulous voices of some few
> Poore brain-sicke men, styl'd *Poets*, here with you,
> Have, with such envie of their graces, sung

> The painted *Beauties* other *Empires* sprung;
> Letting their loose, and winged fictions flie
> To infect all climates, yea our puritie;
> As of one PHAETHON, that fir'd the world,
> And, that, before heedlesse flames were hurld
> About the *Globe,* the *Æthiopes* were as faire,
> As other *Dames;* now blacke, with blacke despaire:
> And in respect of their complections chang'd,
> Are eachwhere, since, for lucklesse creatures rang'd.   (155–66)

These lines draw an unflattering picture of the poet as a disturber of peace. His poetic fiction, which has initiated the quest of the masque, is morally ambiguous from Niger's point of view: it heedlessly spreads an inconvenient truth about the black beauties and plants in them a longing for perfect beauty. But the context of the masque makes it clear that the fiction is not a fiction at all but a fact. The masque praises the court by celebrating its power to vindicate the fiction's factuality, indeed, its power "to make fable true" (to use one of Jonson's compliment formulas). Such perfect beauty not only exists in the white complexion of the English court ladies but also has the power to perfect imperfect beauties.

A satirist's flight from the underworld of London to the world above, the court, is the device of *Mercury Vindicated from the Alchemists at Court,* written in 1616.[16] The flight of Mercury, who emerges as a figure of the satirist in the antimasque, brings about a confrontation of two kinds of art— one serving the underworld, the other the king, an archetypal poet. The masque begins with a song of a Cyclope:

> Soft, subtile fire, thou soul of art,
>   Now do thy part
> On weaker Nature, that through age is lamed.
>   Take but thy time, now she is old,
>   And the Sunne her friend growne cold,
> She will no more, in strife with thee be named.
>
> Looke, but how few confesse her now,
>   In cheeke or browe!
> From every head, almost, how she is frighted!
>   The very age abhorres her so,
>   That it learnes to speake and goe
> As if by art alone it could be righted.   (6–17)

Cyclopes' claim that the alchemists' art is to supersede decaying Nature in her creative function is quickly repudiated by their own patron Mercury, who is now, significantly, their prisoner. Mercury asks the audience to rescue him from their sooty clutch:

Now the place and goodnesse of it protect me. One tender-hearted creature, or other, save *Mercury,* and free him. Ne're an olde Gentle-woman i'the house, that has a wrinckle about her, to hide mee in? I could run into a Serving-womans pocket now; her glove, any little hole. Some mercifull farthingale among so many, be bounteous, and undertake me: I will stand, close, up, any where, to escape this polt-footed *Philosopher,* old *Smug* here of *Lemnos,* and his smoaky familie. (30–38)

His account of the various vexations and mortifications he has suffered in the hands of the alchemists effectively explodes their pretensions to a second Nature. Their forge is activated not by any divine spark but by the hellfire of subterranean London. Art, for them, is that which has utility for procuring bodily comforts: it is to provide victuals, cure bodily disease, and manufacture synthetic gold. Mercury is simply another herring, another oyster, or another cucumber, as their treatments of him testify:

what betweene their salts and their sulfures; their oiles, and their tartars, their brines and their vinegars, you might take me out now a sous'd *Mercury,* now a salted *Mercury,* now a smoak'd and dri'd *Mercury,* now a pouldred and pickl'd *Mercury:* never Herring, Oyster, or Cucumber past so many vexations: my whole life with 'hem hath bene an exercise of torture; one, two, three, foure and five times an hour ha'they made mee dance the *Philosophicall* circle, like an Ape through a hoope, or a dogge in a wheele. I am their turne-spit indeed: They eate or smell no rost-meate but in my name. I am their bill of credit still, that passes for their victuals and house-roome. (50–61)

They believe, reports Mercury, that they can "right" Nature by tinkering with her works:

Marry above here, Perpetuity of beauty, (doe you heare, Ladies) health, Riches, Honours, a matter of Immortality is nothing. They will calcine you a grave matron (as it might bee a mother o' the maides) and spring up a young virgin, out of her ashes, as fresh as a *Phoenix:* Lay you an old Courtier o'the coales like a sausedge, or a bloat-herring, and after they ha'broil'd him enough, blow a soule into him with a paire of bellowes, till he start up into his galliard, that was made when *Mounsieur* was here. They professe familiarly to melt down all the old sinners o'the suburbes once in halfe a yeere, into fresh gamesters againe. Get all the crack'd maiden-heads, and cast 'hem into new Ingots, halfe the wenches o' the town are *Alchemie.* (92–104)

What they promise is nothing less than a perpetual sublimation of the leaden world into something golden—age into youth, and death into immortality. But the squalid process of manufacturing youth and beauty as well as the crude raw materials—human greed, lust, and vanity—betrays the basic moral deficiency of their scheme. In their literal-minded translation of fiction into physical fact, they deform instead of reform the world: instead of beauty and youth they bring into the world monstrous deformities. By fleeing from the alchemists, Mercury flees from their preoccupation with the physical that perverts the transforming power of art.

Significantly, Mercury's account contains startling intimations that the soot of the false art shrouds not only the underworld but also the world above, the court itself. Those intimations become serious charges when they are visualized in the form of Vulcan and his troop of "threadbare alchemists," who claim the patron of art as their captive, and are corroborated by the unhelping, if helpless, audience. Vulcan's assault and the antimasque let loose by him are to be countered by the king, and true alchemy represented by him. The beginning of that contest between true and false art is signaled by Mercury, who appeals directly to the king, identifying him with Sol, the multi-functional symbol of gold, perfect moral nature, and true transforming power: "See, they begin to muster againe, and draw their forces out against me! The *Genius* of the place defend me! You that are both the *Sol* and *Jupiter* of this spheare, *Mercury* invokes your majesty against the sooty Tribe here; for in your favour onely, I growe recover'd and warme" (104–9).

Mercury's next speech is not only a definition of false art but also an active defense of true art and indeed himself. It exposes as fraudulent and ridiculous the Cyclope's initial claim that their fire and art are to replace Sol and Nature in their "great act of generation." In their lame attempt to remake the works of Nature, they only adulterate and spoil her, breeding monsters. The true artist figured in the Sol-king, on the contrary, works with Nature toward the perfection of the world and man. The difference between the two artists is that between deformity and excellence, which will be obvious even to those "who have but their senses":

Art thou not asham'd, *Vulcan,* to offer in defence of thy fire and Art, against the excellence of the Sunne and Nature, creatures more imperfect, then the very flies and insects, that are her trespasses and scapes? Vanish with thy insolence, thou and thy Imposters, and all mention of you melt, before the Majesty of this light, whose *Mercury* henceforth I professe to be, and never again the *Philosophers.* Vanish, I say, that all who have but their senses, may see and judge the difference between thy ridiculous monsters, and his absolute features. (186–95)

Mercury's pledge to be Sol's servant is an indication that he has achieved his quest of true art, and that he has become a panegyrist of the wonder wrought by the king. Upon his banishment of Vulcan's tribe, "the whole Scene changed to a glorious bowre, wherein Nature was placed with Prometheus at her feete; And the twelve Masquers, standing about them" (196–98). The imperfect creatures from Vulcan's forge are replaced by the perfect "creatures of the Sunne" (206). From the brazen world of Vulcan is delivered a golden world of Sol.

What follows is a celebration of Sol's union with Nature. The transformation of the world into something better can be achieved not by outwitting and repudiating but by working in conjunction with Nature. The king's creative potency is nothing if not a reenactment of Nature's alchemy, her natural supernatural art of breeding a golden world. To praise him is to praise Nature, and to praise her is in turn to be a true artist.

By denying the alchemists the title of true artist, Jonson criticizes their attempt to reform the world through a literal translation of fiction into fact. Their pursuit shares much the same niggardly spirit with Plutus, who in *Love Restored* is incapable of measuring the masque's social value in terms other than money. Plutus condemns poetry for its lack of utility, while the alchemists profane it by turning it into mere utility. Jonson, however, does not deny the value of the impulse to actualize fiction itself, or the power of art to change the world of fact. On the contrary, by identifying the king as a neoplatonic Sol, an archetypal poet, he confers on art real moral and political power that can indeed refashion the world of fact into an ideal world. The king, at once an actual person and a symbolic Sol, mediates the real and ideal worlds, naturalizing fiction and fictionalizing fact. The main masque absorbs the criticism of art offered in the antimasque into a vindication of art's higher, and more effective, transforming power.

The masque as an epideictic form imposes on its writer severe limitations: its decorum as a *laus regis* ties him to the rules of compliment if not of flattery.[17] The official fiction of order and harmony is bound to overpower whatever personal perception of the factual world the masque writer has managed to introduce into the world of the masque. By converting a masque into a masque about the masque, Jonson is not only able to examine the problems those restrictions entail but also to free himself from them: whatever tribute he brings to the king is also a tribute to poetry itself. The celebration of the king is a celebration of poetry.

The anti-masque of a typical Jonsonian meta-masque scrutinizes the very premises of masquing. It challenges the authenticity of the masque's vision by exposing its artificiality—its extravagance and its shallow illusionism—in the very act of creating that vision, and it stresses the fragility of the masque world by introducing into it hostile forces, which serve the court audience as reminders of the forgotten time and reality. The tendency of the main masque to detach itself from time and reality in order to mingle with timeless ideals is held in check, and undermined, by the extreme realism of the anti-masque. But the generically ensured triumph of the main masque over the antimasque also assures poetry of its freedom from restrictions of time and reality. The masque's vision does not just overpower the very forces introduced to undermine its authenticity; it is given substance by them. Theatrical illusion is shattered only to reassert itself with redoubled force, much as poetry's transforming power is attacked only to be vindicated and celebrated as a real power.

The problem of how to reconcile fact and fiction, of course, is not peculiar to the epideictic poet. It confronts every writer who tries to express timeless ideals by representing a time-bound world and who strives to give a personal voice to a form constrained by fixed rules. But the "occasional" nature of epideictic poetry—its generic obligation to satisfy the demands of an audience sharply defined in time and place—makes the problem the inevitable focus of the epideictic poet's conscious attention. In his search for a solution to the problem, and as a solution, Jonson frequently turns his epideictic poetry into commentaries on that problem, thus modifying the definition of the genre itself.

5

"Rare Poemes Aske Rare Friends"

The Poet and the Reader in *Epigrammes*

Jonson's recent critics often argue that a deeply rooted suspicion of things in flux is the source of his desire to protect his text, a desire conspicuously expressed in his publication of the 1616 folio *Works*. Jonas Barish, for example, maintains that, because of his ideal of stasis, Jonson was at odds with theater, which by nature is Protean. Barish goes on to say that Jonson's antitheatricalism is nowhere so evident as in the printing of his plays, which was a stratagem to lift them "out of the turbulence of the public arena into the page." Enlarging Barish's thesis, Timothy Murray asserts that Jonson's printing of his plays was meant to effect an "intellectual possession" of theatrical text and thus to turn the "playful dialogue" between the playwright and the audience into a "univocal monologue" of the playwright. Richard C. Newton argues that Jonson's antitheatricalism is a partial expression of his general quest for constancy of text, and that Jonson's printing of *Works* is in effect a "reification of the literary artifact" that discourages the reader's liberty of interpretation.[1]

Indeed, Jonson's 1616 folio *Works* is a monumental gesture against change and fluidity of text, against Time's fell hand, and against the reader's misinterpretation. But the causes, psychological or otherwise, of his desire to gain maximum control over his audience lie deeper, I think, than his fear of change or Puritanical aversion to Protean theater. What does Jonson purport to achieve by silencing the reader on the one hand and by asserting the textuality of his work on the other hand? His troubled relationship with his audience is an inescapable result of his dual allegiance to fact and fiction, which in its turn stems from his faith as a Humanist poet in poetry's obligation to teach and reform the world, whose ideals are by no means the same as his. His struggle to reconcile fact and fiction in his writing is in part an attempt to present the audience with an accurate depiction of the world as he knows it, while minimizing the seductive power of his mimesis. His private attempt to reconcile fact and fiction is transferred to the audience's reception of his representations of the world. The fiction, in this case, is not timeless ideals but the fiction that the readers already have about their world, and the fiction that they make out of the pictures of facts he presents them with. The problem of how to control the audience is part of his problem as an epideictic poet.

Jonson's desire to control his audience stems from his commitment to Renaissance theories of poetry as an educational instrument. The problem of right reading is central to the Renaissance Humanist poetic scheme. As Sidney witnesses in his *Defence of Poetry,* how the reader receives the poem is a crucial issue for a poetic scheme that conceives of the "ending end" of poetry as moving the reader to virtuous action. The success of the entire didactic program depends on the reader's ability to read correctly. Early in the *Defence,* insisting that, unlike building castles in the air, the poet's delivering forth of "the *Idea* or fore-conceit" is not wholly imaginative, Sidney argues, "So far substantially it worketh, not only to make a Cyrus, which had been but a particular excellency as nature might have done, but to bestow a Cyrus upon the world to make many Cyruses, if they will learn aright why and how that maker made him" (79). The poet's making of the poem is substantial, because its effects on the reader are substantial. Xenophon's making of the *Cyropaedia* is substantial and material, because the textual Cyrus, unlike the "natural" particular Cyrus, has the power to generate many Cyruses.[2] And that power, Sidney argues, can be activated only by the reader, who is able to "learn aright" why and how Xenophon made the *Cyropaedia.* The final condition for a successful working of the poem's educative power is the reader's correct reception of the poem. And the ultimate proof that the poet's making of the poem is substantial comes from the reader—that is, from his act of making himself into the thing that the poem figures forth.

Misreading is more than a usual threat for a poetic scheme as dependent upon right reading as this is. Should the reader fail to read correctly, the poet's didactic intention would also fail. And such failure, as Sidney was well aware, does occur. The reader often is incapable of understanding what he reads, like the *mysomousoi* or poet-haters, who misread Agrippa's and Erasmus's jest as earnest (99). Often the reader refuses to act on the knowledge that is given to him through the poem, like the tyrant Alexander Pheraeus, who wept at watching a tragedy yet did not mollify his "hardened heart" (96). And these misreaders, as Margaret W. Ferguson takes Sidney to be implying, are as much abusers of poetry as the poet-apes are. Ferguson argues, rightly I think, that Sidney, in his argument against Plato, uses Plutarch's "How the Young Man Should Study Poetry" in order to suggest that right readers can withstand the potential abuses of poetry—nurturing the passions or confusing fact with fiction. Conversely, by allowing themselves to be swayed by the abused power of poetry, misreaders in effect abuse poetry.[3]

The poet's responsibility, then, is to help, and if need be, to force, the reader to arrive at a correct understanding of the poem. The poet should, in the first place, communicate to the reader what he has to say as unambiguously as possible. One way of doing that is, of course to secure constancy of text. Jonson's quest for stable text is a quest for a device to secure maximum communication of the authorial intention and to reduce the risk of misreading. Needless to say, Jonson's protection of the authorially controlled meaning of text does not stop at placing a physical barrier between what the author has written and what the reader writes in his mind. His devices against misinterpretation are as aggressive as they are diverse.[4]

The right reading, Jonson repeatedly asserts, is discovering the authorial intentions. At the end of the induction to *The Magnetic Lady,* he describes two ways of watching a play: "For, I must tell you, (not out of mine owne *Dictamen,* but the *Authors,*) a good *Play,* is like a skeene of silke, which, if you take by the right end, you may wind off, at pleasure, on the bottome, or card of your discourse, in a tale, or so; how you will: But if you light on the wrong end, you will pull all into a knot, or elf-lock; which nothing but the sheers, or a candle will undoe, or separate" (135–41). One either follows the clue provided by the playwright, finding at the end the authorially intended meaning of the play, or pursues the wrong one, destroying the whole play in the result. Interpreting the play in whatever way one pleases without the guidance of the author is, as Probee argues later in the play, committing a "civill murder" of the play (36).

The misinterpretation Jonson warns against in this particular instance is what he calls the practice of "application," a form of misinterpretation based on the naive assumption that the characters the poet is describing are portraits of contemporary personages. The audience's (or the reader's) credulous confusion of fact and fiction can be a serious threat to the poet: it turns him into a blackmailer, or into a parasite thriving on the vice of others. And for Jonson, who had been accused of blackmail by rivals like Dekker and Marston, such a threat must have been more than real. He suggests that the misinterpreter is not just credulous but actively tyrannous. In the dedicatory epistle prefixed to *Volpone,* he says that those "invading interpreters" who "professe to have a key for deciphering everything . . . cunningly, and often, utter their owne virulent malice, under other mens simplest meanings" (62–67). The misinterpreters see only what they wish to see, and understand only what they wish to understand. They (mis)appropriate, distort, and remake the poet's work according to their own purposes. They deny the poet the right to control the meaning of his own words, imposing their own meaning on what he says, what he writes. Their disregard and distortion of the authorial intention, Jonson suggests in *Sejanus,* are as unjust and destructive as Sejanus's "Furious enforcing, most unjust presuming, / Malicious, and manifold applying, / Foul wresting, and impossible construction" (3.227–29) of the realities of the Romans' words and deeds. It is a form of tyranny.

This fear of tyrannous misinterpreters affects every aspect of Jonson's work as a whole. Indeed, his characteristic self-reflexiveness is an active form of warning against fictions the reader creates with his writings: he exposes the artificiality of his work in order to prevent the reader's uncritical acceptance of his mimesis as factual; he directly warns against misreading in his writings—prefaces, addresses to the reader, dedicatory epistles, prologues, epilogues, and "editorial" poems and plays. And his concern with the accurate interpretation of his work explains in part why he uses the same words and the same motifs in various works: repetition is a defense not only against miscommunication but also against misinterpretation.[5]

It is only with apprehensiveness that Jonson releases a work from his protective hands to the uncertain world inhabited by "lay" as well as "learned" readers.[6] In an epigram to Alphonso Ferabosco, he dwells on the helplessness of a work of art once it has entered the world and become a common property of all readers:

> When we doe give, ALPHONSO, to the light,
>   A worke of ours, we part with our owne right;
> For, then, all mouthes will judge, and their owne way:
>   The learn'd have no more priviledge, then the lay.
>   (*Epigrammes* 131, "To the Same," 1–4)

Against the uninstructed censures of Court Witlings, against the mental rewritings of Groom Idiots, Jonson sets out to defend his poetry. His first recourse is to the reader's critical understanding. In the first of the *Epigrammes,* he appeals "To the Reader": "Pray thee, take care, that tak'st my booke in hand, / To reade it well: that is, to understand" (1–2). A critical reader is the best protection against misreading.[7] Jonson, however, never wholly relegates to the reader the task of successful communication. Even while he is limiting his readership to understanders, he devises ways to secure maximum communication of his meaning and thus to circumscribe the range of the reader's interpretative activity. The chief device Jonson uses for that purpose is repetition, both lexical and thematic. Jonson's most carefully edited volume of poetry, the *Epigrammes,* provides numerous examples of the device: he uses again and again certain solitary words, rhyming pairs, and phrases, and repeatedly addresses the same particular persons and types.

Repetition, it should be noted, has been recognized as a basic device against misunderstanding. Such figures of word repetition as *anaphora, antistrophe, ploce, climax,* and *antistasis,* familiar to any Renaissance writer or orator, are essentially means of attaining emphasis. Modern communication theorists also attest the effectiveness of repetition as a communicational tool. Noting writers' heavy reliance on redundancy as a stratagem to achieve clarity and eloquence, Liane Norman argues that misunderstanding which is likely to occur in any linguistic transaction is countered by the "built-in propensity of language to operate redundantly." Redundancy is a form of "insurance against misunderstanding" and "the agent of the reader's drawing the correct conclusions."[8]

Throughout the *Epigrammes,* abstract words like *great* (157 times), *good* (136 times), *name* (90 times), *virtue* (76 times), *fame* (70 times), *word* (49 times), *fortune* (39 times), *sense* (34 times), *birth* (22 times), *show* (22 times), *conscience* (18 times), *shame* (18 times), and *merit* (12 times) reappear like leitmotifs. A good example of Jonson's use of these single words is the epigram "On Don Surly" (*Epigrammes* 28), in which *great* occurs fourteen times in twenty-two lines:

> Don Surly, to aspire the glorious name
> Of a *great* man, and to be thought the same,
> Makes serious use of all *great* trade he knowes.
> He speakes to men with a *Rhinocerotes* nose,
> Which hee thinkes *great;* and so reades verses, too:
> And, that is done, as he saw *great* men doe.
> H'has tympanies of businesse, in his face,
> And, can forget mens names, with a *great* grace.
> He will both argue, and discourse in oathes,
> Both which are *great.* And laugh at ill-made clothes;
> That's *greater,* yet: to crie his owne up neate.
> He doth, at meales, alone, his pheasant eate,
> Which is maine *greatnesse.* And, at his still boord,
> He drinkes to no man: that's, too, like a lord.
> He keepes anothers wife, which is a spice
> Of solemne *greatnesse.* And he dares, at dice,
> Blaspheme god, *greatly:* Or some poore hinde beat,
> That breathes in his dogs way: and this is *great.*
> Nay more, for *greatnesse* sake, he will be one
> May heare my *Epigrammes,* but like of none.

> Surly, use other arts, these only can
> Stile thee a most *great* foole, but no *great* man.
>
> (emphasis mine)

The sheer abundance of occurrences of the word *great* ensures the reader's attention to the word itself. But the repetition at work here is not simply a static device of emphasis. It serves as a chief vehicle for the poem's satiric intention. Through the repetition of *great*, Jonson is able to expose Don Surly's moral blindness, which is reflected in his incapability to recognize the multiplicity of meanings of *great*: "great" as "good" is wholly lost to this Don, who tries to acquire the "name / Of a great man" by imitating the vicious manners of grandees. The gap between what Don Surly takes to be greatness and what greatness ideally means ever widens at each repetition of the word *great*. The volume of vice swells to "greatnesse" as the volume of virtue dwindles to nothingness. The result is an anatomy of Don Surly's guilt, which reduces him to a bundle of words, all mimicking each other's sound. Jonson's last verdict on the guilty Don, "these only can / Stile thee a most great foole, but no great man," becomes something of an oracle spoken in a "desperate soelecisme" of the word *great*.

Repetition of words provides links between the poems in the *Epigrammes*. The word *great* in its last appearance in this poem is negatively defined by its previous appearances therein: someone who does what Don Surly does is "no great man." What happens in this particular poem happens in the whole collection. This poem provides part of the context in which the famous epigram "On Lucy Countesse of Bedford" should be read: Jonson finds in her an ideal woman, whose "greatest bloud" is "more good then great," and who is free from "that solemne vice of greatnesse, pride." Greatness becomes truly great only when it is synonymous with goodness, as is the greatness of Lucy, Countess of Bedford.

Like *great* and *good*, recurrent words often occur in significant pairs: *name* pairs with *fame* or *shame*, *fortune* with *merit* or *virtue*, *birth* with *honor* or *virtue*, *show* with *conscience*, and *word* with *sense*. These pairs constitute the basic idioms of Jonson's language of praise and blame in the *Epigrammes*. In the epigrams of praise the two component words of each pair are inter-changeable, but when the two appear in an ironic context they become terms of dispraise. The case in point is the pair *name/fame*, which serves as Jonson's most explicit means of expressing his positive and negative ideals for man and society, as many of his critics have noted.[9] A good man's "name" is a direct index to his character, as Sir Horace Vere's name literally is:

> Which of thy names I take, not onely beares
> A *romane* sound, but *romane* vertue weares:
> Illustrous VERE, or HORACE; fit to be
> Sung by a HORACE, or a *Muse* as free;

> Which thou art to thy selfe: whose fame was wonne
>   In th'eye of *Europe,* where thy deeds were done,
> When on thy trumpet shee did sound a blast,
>   Whose rellish to eternitie shall last.
>
> (*Epigrammes* 91, "To Sir Horace Vere," 1–8)

Sir Horace Vere, who won his "fame" through his deeds, is Sir Horace "Truly" ("Vere" Englished), since his "deeds" are his own muse, a Horace. This perfect correspondence between "name" and "fame" has an antitype in the satiric epigram "To Person Guiltie" (*Epigrammes* 30):

> Guiltie, be wise; and though thou know'st the crimes,
>   Be thine, I taxe, yet doe not owne my rimes:
> 'Twere madnesse in thee, to betray thy *fame,*
>   And person to the world; ere I thy *name.*
>
> (1–4; emphasis mine)

In Jonson's satiric epigrams, as here, the correspondence between "fame" and "name" takes away a person's name and leaves a term of shame instead: a guilty person's name and fame are all "Guiltie." It is from repetition of the same pair of words in two entirely different contexts—one of praise, and the other of blame—that the reader comes to understand the value system Jonson tries to teach throughout the epigrams. The positive and negative correlation between "name" and "fame" are two expressions of a single ideal, the exact correspondence between word and thing.

Through repeated use of the same monosyllabic words the poet asserts his presence, invading, and reigning over, the reader's ears and mind with his voice, so that the reader, even if he be a Groom Idiot whose "ignorance still laughs in the wrong place" (*Epigrammes* 58) or a Person Guilty who habitually "perverts" his sense (*Epigrammes* 38), cannot misunderstand what he says. By insistently repeating the same words, Jonson tries to limit the reader's range of interpretation, as if he wants to exact from the reader the echo of his own voice with minimum alteration.

Jonson uses not only the same words but also the same subjects over and over. Of the thirty-nine actual persons praised in the *Epigrammes,* twelve are addressed more than once, and of forty-seven vicious types, seven are treated more than once.[10] By repeatedly looking at the same persons and types (and by making the reader do so), Jonson defines and redefines "all vertues, and their Contraries" to arrive at and to transmit to the reader the "exact knowledge" of them (*Discoveries,* H&S 8:595).

Jonson arranged ten of the nineteen groups of poems addressed to the same person, or the same vicious type, into pairs, providing the title "To the Same" for the second poem of each pair. The pairs so made often function as an extended epigram in two parts: the first describes a particular fact or poses a problem; the second comments on it, often in general terms, teaching the reader how to read and understand the first. The two epigrams on Sir Henry Goodyer provide an example. In Epigram 85 Jonson attempts to find in his friend-patron's "few days' sport" some moral significance. He turns a casual exercise in falconry into a study of ideal human behavior by discerning in the hawk an emblem of an ideal intellectual activity. The bird soars toward knowledge and strikes ignorance. Turning a hawk into an emblem of intellectual activity is extended to the turning of a friend into a book. In Epigram 86 Jonson's reading of Sir Henry Goodyer's "pleasures" turns out to be an imitation of what he praises his friend-reader for: Goodyer makes "[his] friends bookes, and [his] bookes friends." The specific instance of "reading" a friend, presented in the first epigram, is glossed in the second epigram in more abstract terms:

> When I would know thee Goodyere, my thought lookes
> Upon thy wel-made choise of friends, and bookes;
> Then doe I love thee, and behold thy ends
> In making thy friends bookes, and thy bookes friends: (1–4)

In poems addressed to the same person but not arranged in pairs, Jonson examines the subject of his praise and blame from more than one perspective. John Donne, for example, becomes a book that should be read more than once. Epigram 23, the first of the two epigrams addressed to Donne, is somewhat abstract, if comprehensive: Jonson recognizes Donne as a supreme poet, "the delight of PHOEBUS, and each *Muse*," whose poetry springs not merely from his "wit" but from his "best life," and whose incomparable worth as a good man and poet he can praise only by leaving off praising. He says he wants to praise Donne for his

> language, letters, arts, best life,
> Which might with halfe mankind maintayne a strife.
> All which I meant to praise, and, yet, I would;
> But leave, because I cannot as I should!   (7–10)

The inarticulate praise assumes a confident voice when he undertakes a rereading to give locality to Donne's ethical attributes by defining his own place relative to the supreme poet. In Epigram 96, "To John Donne," he finds Donne a model critic and reader, who is discriminating in his choice of praiseworthy poems and plain-speaking in his censure of the blameworthy, most unlike the "Censorious Courtling," who damns with faint praise (*Epigrammes* 52). To submit his poems to such a reader as Donne is to distinguish himself from a herd of common poets, who "for claps do write," and whom "Pui'nees, porters, players, praise delight" (9–10). With this assessment of

Donne's worth, Jonson (and thus the reader) arrives at a more exact knowledge of Donne: Donne is a good man, poet, and reader.

In his second address to Donne, Jonson reaches a fuller understanding not only of his subject but also of his own poetic power to identify and bear witness to virtue. Sending his poems to Donne and writing on that occasion is an act of sealing his own title as "a Poet" before the eyes of the reader: "Who shall doubt, DONNE, where I a poet bee, / When I dare send my *Epigrammes* to thee?" (1–2). Jonson's praise of the subject merges into a praise of himself.

Throughout the *Epigrammes,* Jonson reminds the reader of his presence not only by repeating the same words and subjects but also by intruding himself into the poems with proclamations of his worth.

Jonson's mistrust of the reader as a potential misunderstander has its counterpart in his presentation of himself as a legitimate poet. If the fate of the poem in the reader's hand is uncertain for the poet, the poet's motive in producing the poem can be dubious to the reader. If the reader can construe the poem after his own fashion, independent of the authorial intention, the poet can easily slip into subservience to the undisciplined palate of the ignorant multitude. The moral purpose of his poem can better be served if the poet can clear himself of such charges of subservience. He must establish his probity as well as his wisdom; he must persuade the reader with his character as well as with his voice, since, as one of Jonson's gleanings from Vives tells us,

> The two chiefe things that give a man reputation in counsell, are the opinion of his *Honesty;* and the opinion of his *Wisdom:* The authority of those two will perswade, when the same Counsels, utter'd by other persons lesse qualified, are of no efficacy, or working.
>
> *Wisedome* without *Honesty* is meere craft, and coosinage. And therefore the reputation of Honesty must first be gotten; which cannot be, but by living well. A good life is a maine Argument. (*Discoveries, H&S* 8:565–66)

Persuasion by character (*ethos*) is of course a commonplace of Aristotelian rhetoric: "Of the modes of persuasion supplied by the speech itself there are three kinds. The first kind reside in the character [*ethos*] of the speaker; the second consist in producing a certain [the right] attitude in the hearer; the third appertain to the argument proper, in so far as it actually or seemingly demonstrates."[11] Like the orator, the didactic poet must control the reader's attitude toward the world the poem represents; he must make him accept his version of the truth of things. Like the orator, the poet must "reign in mens affections . . . invade, and break upon them" and make "their minds the thing he writes" (*Discoveries, H&S* 8:587–88). The chief methods Jonson uses to achieve ethical persuasion are assertion of his honesty, attack on the dishonest, identification of himself with the praised, and engagement of the reader in the praise.

The reader of the *Epigrammes* is presented by turns with caveats about the art of reading well and threats to plagiarists and bad poets. Demands made on the reader are justified and reinforced by self-advertisement of the poet as a person of probity. Epigrams 1 and 2 provide a paradigm of Jonson's manipulation of the reader. In Epigram 2, "To My Booke," which follows the directive "To the Reader" in Epigram 1, Jonson makes it clear what kind of poetry he is offering:

> It will be look'd for, booke, when some but see
> Thy title, Epigrammes, and nam'd of mee,
> Thou should'st be bold, licentious, full of gall,
> Wormewood and sulphure, sharpe, and tooth'd withall;
> Become a petulant thing, hurle inke, and wit,
> As mad-men stones: not caring whom they hit.
> Deceive their malice, who could wish it so.
> And by thy wiser temper, let men know
> Thou art not covetous of least selfe-fame,
> Made from the hazard of anothers shame:
> Much lesse with lewd, prophane, and beastly phrase,
> To catch the worlds loose laughter, or vaine gaze.   (1–12)

His defense of poetry becomes an *apologia pro vita sua* in the last two lines of the poem: "He that departs with his owne honesty / For vulgar praise, doth it too dearly buy" (13–14). By distinguishing himself from the bad poets and witlings abusing poetry for the promotion of lust, and by presenting himself as a voice of truth, honesty, and authentiticity, Jonson attempts to shape the reader's attitude toward his poems.

Jonson's numerous *apologiae pro vita sua* hang on the claim of honesty in praise, of the "truth of Argument." To paraphrase Sidney, so far from affirming nothing, the poet affirms only what is already there "and therefore never lieth." The existence of virtue is a fact, not a poetic dream. To praise the virtuous like Robert, Earl of Salisbury, the poet needs only to point, calling them by their names (*Epigrammes* 43):

> What need hast thou of me? or of my *Muse*,
> Whose actions so themselves doe celebrate;
> Which should thy countries love to speake refuse,
> Her foes enough would fame thee, in their hate.
> 'Tofore, great men were glad of *Poets:* Now,
> I, not the worst, am covetous of thee.
> Yet dare not, to my thought, least hope allow
> Of adding to thy fame; thine may to me,

> When, in my booke, men read but CECILL'S name,
> And what I write thereof find farre and free
> From servile flatterie (common *Poets* shame)
> As thou stand'st cleere of the necessitie.

Not praising, but naming. Not describing, but conjuring up the image of Cecil's worthy self through the power of his name. To praise a person is in a sense to identify oneself with him, because the praiser's freedom from "servile flatterie" can only be defended by the praised's freedom from its need. This interdependence between the praiser and the praised is one reason why Jonson often presents himself as possessing the same ethical qualities he attributes to the praised, or why in Jonson's poetry a praise of virtue so often merges with a praise of the poet, who finds himself unable to "lie dumb or hid / To so true worth" (*Epigrammes* 63, "To Robert Earle of Salisburie," 11–12).

What needs to be celebrated is not only the virtue itself but also the poet's power to identify it. And that power is something the reader-understander is challenged to share in the last four lines of the epigram: the reader too can participate in the poet's celebration as a judge of his honesty. The praiser, the praised, and the reader are linked to each other in a chain of interdependency. The praiser judges the praised as praiseworthy, and in turn is judged by the reader. And it is the reader that confers a "legitimate fame" (*Epigrammes* 17, "To the Learned Critick") on the poet and through him on his subject.

In the addresses to the reader prefixed to *Catiline,* Jonson distinguishes three kinds of readers—the reader in ordinary, the reader extraordinary, and the ideal reader, the dedicatee. Jonson describes the reader in ordinary as the one most likely to misread what his poem says. The majority of readers are such, because most people "comment out of affection, selfe tickling, an easinesse, or imitation," not judging "out of knowledge. That is the trying faculty." To the reader extraordinary Jonson's address is brief: "You I would understand to be the better Man, though / Places in Court go otherwise: to you I submit my selfe, and worke. Farewell." But the ideal reader does more than understand. He judges with "that great and singular faculty of judgement" and vindicates "truth." And by so doing he countenances a "legitimate Poeme." The reader's responsibility is no less than giving the sanction of truth and immortality to the poem and the poet—a judge of truth.

The importance of being the right kind of reader can be further illustrated by the fact that the identification of his subject as a good reader is one of Jonson's highest terms of praise. The great goodness Jonson finds in his poem to "Lucy, Countesse of Bedford, with Mr. Donne's Satires" (*Epigrammes* 94) is her "learned and manly soul," because she is hospitable to the poet's need to be understood. And by achieving the ultimate distinction of being a good reader, Lucy becomes something more than that. She is a patron of muses, "The muses' evening-as their morning-star" (16).

But if the reader fails to fulfill his part, the result is grievous to both the reader and the poet. It reduces the reader to a Mere Censurer, or a Groom Idiot, the poet to a poet-prostitute, and the poet's praise to flattery, which Jonson describes in *Discoveries* as "the honey distilling from a whorish voice; which is not praise, but poyson" (*H&S* 8:596–97). Jonson represents himself as a person of integrity not only to give moral authority to his instruction, but also to invite the reader's active participation in the weighty business of protecting and propagating "truth, and libertie" (Dedicatory Epistle "To the Great Example of Honor and Vertue, The Most Noble William Earle of Pembroke," 16).[12]

But how is it possible for the reader to do his duty? One answer lies in Jonson's concern to control the reader's attitude toward his poems. Jonson's repetition of words and subjects is aimed at training the reader's sense-making activity: he programs, as it were, the reader's ears and eyes to the voice of the surface text. And when he invites the reader to participate in truth making, he demands that the reader read and understand his whole person, the very stuff the poem's subtext is made of. Jonson's demand can best be satisfied by those who are already his friends, sharing with him the same ideals as well as the same codes of communication.[13] It is after all to John Selden, who is "truly able to know" his "speciall Worth," that Jonson can say "I know to whom I write. Here, I am sure, / Though I am short, I cannot be obscure" (*Underwood* 14, "An Epistle to Master John Selden," 1–2).[14] He is the kind of reader who knows how to supply the gaps left by the poet, and how to illuminate the area of meaning that for other "readers" dims into obscurity when it is not explicitly stated. Jonsonian truth is a product of the collaboration between the reader and the poet. Jonson's ideal reader is ultimately himself. He demands that the reader acquire his language and become his other self. Only then can the reader perform his part in perpetuating Jonson and poetry, which are one.

Jonson's act of enclosing the readership within the community of friends of his soul calls, paradoxically for a poet, for a silence, an eloquent silence punctuated with small gestures and significant monosyllabic words. The two apparently incompatible urges—one to protect the purity of his voice from the meddling world, the other to sing aloud and teach the world—achieve a precarious equilibrium in the fiction of an ideal readership, a small community of understanders. Examined from this point of view, Jonson's "publicness" is only minimally public; he represents the few who are extensions of himself. In his poetry, art dissolves into life, eloquence into silence, public occasion into poetic occasion, the praised into the praiser, and the reader into "the Poet," who sings, but does so "high and aloof, / Safe from the wolf's black jaw, and the dull ass's hoof" (*Underwood* 23, "An Ode. To Himselfe," 135–36).

Conclusion: Jonson's Literary Dialectic of Ideal and History

One of Jonson's most engaging commentaries on the problem of representation is *Underwood* 52, a poem made of a pair of epistles, "A Poem sent me by Sir William Burlase. The Painter to the Poet" and "My Answer. The Poet to the Painter." In the first epistle, Burlase speaks of the painter's difficulty in depicting visibly the inner qualities of a person, namely, Ben's "worth" (1), which the senses do not directly apprehend but reason still comprehends. In order to compensate for this failure, the painter tries another art—the art of verbal portraiture. But even with this art the painter finds himself unable to encompass Ben's worth. A totally comprehensive representation is not possible: "There's no Expression" (12).

In "My Answer," Jonson replies to Burlase by relating the problem of representation to that of praising. In the first two stanzas of the epistle, he punningly suggests that the real difficulty the painter has is not so much how to portray his inner worth as how to contain his enormous physical "worth" in a small canvas. The task of containing the huge matter of Ben within the narrow confines of Burlase's canvas entails a process of modification and idealization of all that the eye sees. But Jonson argues that if the painter attempts to remake and idealize his imperfect appearance in conformity with conventions of portraiture, he will create something other than he is, a fictional image:

> But whilst you curious were to have it be
> An *Archetype,* for the world to see,
> You made it a brave piece, but not like me.   (13–15)

But in the rest of the poem Jonson claims that his own verbal portrait in "Black and white" (20) *can* capture the inner qualities of a person, precisely because it is free from far-fetched idealization of fact, a liability the visual art is susceptible to with its "flattering colours, or false light" (20–21). To draw the "face" (22) of friendship he will simply write the name of his friend: he "will write *Burlase*" (24). Through this act of naming Burlase, Jonson makes the actual express the ideal: friendship becomes Burlase, and Burlase friendship. "*Burlase*" portrays at once the idea of friendship and the particular friend. Both the problem of representation and its related one of praising are resolved at the same time, because when the actual person is an embodiment of an abstract moral idea, a description of the actual is an expression of the ideal, and terms of description become terms of praise.

"My Answer" belongs to the genre of "instructions to the painter," a minor genre originating in the rivalry between the sisters arts, poetry and painting, in terms of which a "rethinking of the relation between language and 'reality' " was conducted within Renaissance poetics, according to Howard Felperin.[1] Jonson uses the genre's typical attention to the problem of representation as the occasion to examine his own epideictic art. The problems of representation and praising that he explores as the painter's in the first half of the poem turn out in the second half to be also his. As a praiser of an actual person, he shares with the portrait painter the problem of how to express the ideal through a medium traditionally regarded as descriptive of the actual—or to put it in another way, how to praise and yet be faithful to the world of facts. Jonson's "Answer" resolves the epideictic poet's problem without really solving it. By asserting that in this case to represent is to praise, he moves away from the problem of praising; by calling his friend into the poem, he replaces representation with life itself and thus cancels the problem of representation. But in leaving off representing and praising, he sends the reader back to life, in effect relegating to him the task of completing his poem and his praise, something that only those who know the unrepresented story of the real-life Burlase, and thus know how to listen to the poet's language of silence, can adequately perform.

How are we to take this way of resolving the problem by canceling it? What motives are we to attribute to the poet in this? How are we to interpret the competition between life and representation in attaining totality, the source of tension in both epistles? How are we to take the defeat of representation in that rivalry with life, which the poet seems to admit in the topos of modesty and the act of naming? What does Jonson mean by relying on the reader so heavily? What we do with these questions depends, I think, on our conception of the relationship between literature and life in the Renaissance and also in our time. I think this is so especially because epideictic poetry acknowledges its roots in the realities of experience—actual persons and events—more expressly than any other poetic kind. It has life itself as a measure of the sincerity and truthfulness of what it professes and represents. It is "historical poetry." And it is precisely in its ambiguous status as historical poetry, or poetical history, that epideictic poetry can be a testing ground for ideas and theories of the problematic relationship between fact and fiction, art and society: as history, it is expected to record and describe realities of experiences which as poetry it transforms and idealizes. Jonson's epideictic poetry in particular thrives on the tension between fact and fiction inherent in the genre. His poems of praise often draw the reader's attention to the mimetic process through which fact is transformed into poetic fiction, and thus constitute as a whole a particularly suggestive commentary on the relationship between literature and life, poetry and history.

Not only its generic dependence upon life but also its proliferation into other forms of Renaissance literary discourse, both social and familiar, renders epideictic poetry a test case of theories of poetry, especially those that emphasize the indissoluble interrelationship between literature and life. The epideictic impulse operates, in varying degrees, in almost every Renaissance literary form, including hymn, epic, pastoral, satire, comedy, tragedy, pageant, and masque, as well as verse epistle. Even Renaissance biography and historiography are essentially epideictic. As O. B. Hardison and Brian Vickers have already noted, and as new historical interpreters of the politics of representation would surely agree, the epideictic impulse characterizes Renaissance literary activities.[2] That is, the problem of how to represent particular facts in epideictic terms must have been endemic not only to those who had to write about an actual person on an actual occasion, but to all writers of the Renaissance. In that sense, an interpretation of the way Jonson handles the problem acquires wider significance as giving access to a better understanding of the Renaissance and the poetry it produced.

The new historicist critics would argue that Jonson's epideictics bear the traces of pressures and constraints he had to deal with as one who was inevitably caught in a web of "relations of power."[3] Discussing Jonson's poetry in relation to the absolutist self-representation of James I, in his *James I and the Politics of Literature*, Jonathan Goldberg, for example, characterizes the poet's career as that of "contained rebellion." He argues that "Jonson found self-justification in his royalist position. . . . The good king's service involves extending himself to society as an exemplar and as the embodiment of desire. He is the fact that words find out, making them true, making the people's voice God's. The chain of command is one of re-presentation. Royalist tenets become the principles of Jonson's poetics." He concludes that, "not an ideologue like Donne, Jonson is nonetheless a representative voice—perhaps the representative voice—of Jacobean culture, creating its language and being created by it, the voice that most fully reproduces his society. . . . Instrumentality, unlike Donne's submission, points to the nature of Jonson's engagement and activity in society, produced and reproduced in his language."[4]

This argument might seem to allow the poet the power to shape his language. But Goldberg's picture of the English Renaissance is a re-presentation of Stephen Greenblatt's—no less deterministic for the different name he gives it.[5] Like that under the Tudors, the world under James I fostered and often engendered duplicitous words—those words forever in defense of themselves. It was the kind of society that so totally controls its individual members that it contains, and sublimates into complicity, even their gestures toward contest and subversion. Goldberg's initial assumption that language and politics are mutually constitutive applies only to the king's language, since the poet's representation does not shape but is always shaped by the king's representation. Thus the negative examples that figure so conspicuously in "To Penshurst" are not "attacks on society, but a register of its sustaining conditions." The bounty of the estate and the family is "a sustained image of royal bounty," and the poem itself "reproduces the sustaining terms of his society."[6] Whatever social realities he registers in his poem, they do nothing but valorize the existing social conditions to the benefit of the king. In short, Jonson, in this poem as elsewhere, is the articulator of the king's rhetoric. The king appropriated language entirely to himself.[7] This interpretation, like Greenblatt's of the Renaissance under the Tudors, deconstructs the image of the Sidneian poet, questioning his ability to penetrate the workings of society and minimizing his potential, if not his intention, to achieve in actuality as well as in poetry a measure of distance and independence from his socio-political situations.

Apart from the role played by James I's absolutist propaganda, the web the king's language weaved, Goldberg almost wholly disregards the roles of historical circumstances in producing the poet's words. This lacuna in his theory of the Renaissance is being filled in more recent studies by revisionist historians of Renaissance literature, which include among others Arthur Marotti's series of studies of the Renaissance patronage system in relation to Elizabethan sonnet sequences and John Donne's poetry, and Annabel Patterson's examination of the impact of censorship on the conditions of writing and reading in early modern England.

In his "John Donne and the Rewards of Patronage," Marotti argues that "the term 'literature of patronage' should not be limited to complimentary dedications designed to get financial and social favors, for almost all English Renaissance literature is a literature of patronage." He goes on to suggest that Donne's discomfort with the patronage system accounts for some peculiarities of his complimentary poems, which "threaten to subvert their conventions, if not the complimentary mode itself."[8] This argument is suggestive for an understanding not only of "coterie poets" like Sidney and Donne but of more professedly public poets like Spenser and Jonson, insofar as it takes cognizance of one important element of what must have been the poets' mixed motives in writing complimentary poetry of an idealizing and stylizing tendency. Patronage royal, aristocratic, and municipal was certainly *one* of the determinants of Jonson's epideictic methods, as his poems about the problem of overpraise suggest. According to Robert C. Evans, another interpreter of the patronage factor in Renaissance production of poetry, Jonson was tied to the rules and constraints of the society's structure of patronage, not only in his public poems but even in his epistles to his friends and "Sons."[9] Indeed, Jonson's idealism itself, Marotti suggests, was fueled with his passionate belief in "the possibility of winning social status through artistic merit."[10] Here, as in Greenblatt/Goldberg's Renaissance, the poet is something merely symptomatic of his economic and political conditions.

Greenblatt/Goldberg's more general and Marotti's more particular deconstruction of the archetypal poet and his social role as Sidney conceives them in *A Defense of Poetry* seems to be coming to a halt with Annabel Patterson's *Censorship and Interpretation: The Conditions of Writing and Reading in Early Modern England*. Arguing that the social and political function of literature was still active in the early modern period, Patterson claims that institutionalized censorship was the crucial factor that determined the conditions of writing and reading in the period.[11] To circumvent censhorship, writers developed "codes of communication" to comment on important matters of public concern. And readers (often including censors) decoded them, joining writers in their effort to keep literature in its "privileged position of compromise" between the magistrates and the governed.[12] She maintains that such Gramscian dissemination of sociopolitical commentary was what the *Underwood* lyrics were intended to achieve. And those include not only the ones written for such great public figures of the Elizabethan and Jacobean state as Sir Walter Raleigh, Francis Bacon, or James Fitzgerald, Earl of Desmond but also the defiantly private one "An Ode: To Himselfe."[13] The codes used in that dissemination were and still are "History," or rather versions of facts about the Jacobean state available to the reader but made absent from the texts of the poems.

Despite its emphasis on the poet's effort to escape the censor's eye, Patterson's "hermeneutics of censorship" is based on the same assumptions about language and society that operate in the Greenblatt/Goldberg paradigm of Renaissance representation of power. The meaning of a text is for her, as for them, indeterminate, ambiguous, and equivocal till "History" intercedes to stabilize it. Her history, like theirs, is a story of material relations and power.

Her Renaissance England, like theirs, is shaped by a highly repressive and highly inclusive sociopolitical system, which could engender and foster only a certain kind of discourse. Whatever different sociopolitical system these new historical critics of Renaissance literature foreground as the determinant of the Renaissance individually, they are united in their conclusion (and their assumption) that in the Renaissance dissimulation was the mode of life and equivocation and defensive irony the mode of discourse. The system, something of a Frankenstein's monster, once brought into being through human agency, began to assert its indomitable will as a universal prison-house keeper. If he was not wholly submissive, the poet was able to exert a modicum of power in contesting the system through exploiting the indeterminacy and the self-deconstructing tendency of language, the kind of power that only emphasizes his essential powerlessness. In this new historicist paradigm, there seems to be little room indeed for the possibilities that some poets might have understood and reacted to the system in ways different from the one deducible from the paradigm—reproducing the king, exploiting patronage, and eluding censorship through mutual indirection, displacement, sublimation, duplicity.[14]

Because of his role as a celebrator of public figures in the Jacobean court, Jonson occupies a prominent place in current discussions of the politics of English Renaissance representation. In fact, he seems to offer a particularly fitting example of the predicament of a poet who has to work with duplicitous words in a duplicitous world, because he is a poet of many contradictions. A sometime bricklayer, he claimed for himself the right of the *Poet* to be a counselor to the king. He seems to have adored some public figures as passionately as he scorned some others. He seems to have known the classical world as intimately as London. He advocated Baconian empiricism but impressed William Drummond as "oppressed with fantasie" (*Conversations, H&S* 1:151.692). He used, but modified and redefined, received conventions of traditional literary genres. His poems often subvert what they ostensibly profess in order to include a larger view of the world than their immediate occasions dictated. He was deeply implicated in the things he condemned in his satires; after all, he was an inveterate eulogist, a client of court partonage, and a popular playwright despite all his vituperative complaints about the audience.[15] Taking what he says in his work at face value would be only a manifest symptom of one's dangerous gullibility. But to dismiss what he says in favor of unspoken words and concealed motives seems to me suspiciously near to committing the unforgivable sin of transferring one's own bad faith to others. In so doing, we give the writer's unconscious or unacknowledged intention too much attention and his declared intention too little, creating thus a new kind of text as univocal as the one it supplants. In so doing, too, we surrender the poet to the all-enveloping system and sanction that system as a fact, not only of the past but very much of our own time.

Jonson's manifold effort to stabilize the contexts his poetry should be read in, I think, should warrant close attention to his more explicit expressions and their particularities, which are after all what make him and his poetry distinctive. To respect his caution against the practice of "application," (mis)interpreting the events and characters the poet describes as direct imitations of contemporary events and persons, is no denial of the specific historicity of his poetic texts.[16] And to say that a literary text is not a historical document is no denial of the textuality of history in general. But what a poetic text includes are not only facts, or facts displaced, but also the ways in which the poet fictionalizes fact, the ways in which he negotiates with his problematic situations, and the ways in which he creates another order of fact through fiction. Examinations of the broad cultural significances of a literary text cannot replace examinations of its particularities, of the specific authorial intention in making the text as it is, and of the impact they together have on the reader.

Jonson's poems of praise bear traces of the historical circumstances of their genesis, traces of the diverse interactions between history and ideal, fact and fiction—in their topical allusions, in their claim of factuality, in their justification of idealization as a didactic device, and in the tension between fact and fiction such claims and justifications indicate. Jonson's foregrounding of the process through which he mediates the actual and the ideal as the real concern of his epideictic poetry is in itself a device to preserve the historicity and particularity of his poetic subjects and his poetic world. But what those traces finally articulate, I think, is not the all-inclusive system but the individual voice of a poet fiercely guarding his intellectual independence against those that make it precarious. In that sense, and to that extent, they show the ways in which he confronts and transforms his immediate circumstances. To explore those ways is to explore the possibility not only that poetry can be history, but that intellectual independence can be achieved in a most restrictive structure.

I opened this chapter by demonstrating that in the poem answering Burlase, Jonson turns the actual friend into an embodiment of friendship. In that face of friendship he portrays, traces of the particular person Burlase are blurred and all but defaced. Diverse historical pressures, which we now have no means to reconstruct, must have played diverse roles in determining the method of praise in this poem. And Jonson opted for transforming the particular into something less particular and more general, something less historically specific and more abstract. But to suppose that the pressures were all socioeconomic, or sociopolitical, is as reductive as to emphasize conventions of a literary form as the primary determinant. The poet chooses literary forms and literary conventions partly because of social pressures, but partly because of the potentialities he finds in those forms and conventions to counteract—confront, transform—the pressures. The product of that encounter between poetry and society is the textual features peculiar to the particular poet, those which most show his individuality. Although idealization is a conventional epideictic method, the path Jonson takes in "My Answer" to reach an idealized picture of the actual friend is entirely his own. By dwelling on the problem of representation and praising even before he starts praising, he invites the reader to consider the gaps that might exist between the actual and the ideal, fact and fiction. By replacing representation with life, he gives the status of fact to the idealized image of Burlase. By insisting on the factual bases of his praise, he again invites a comparison between the world of experience and the world of poetry. But by inviting such a comparison, Jonson indicates the necessity and at the same time the possibility to reshape the actual world in its idealized image that he presents it with.

In insisting on the factuality of his highly idealized image of human nature, Jonson exploits the subversive and the utopian potential of poetry of praise that has long been recognized by both classical and Renaissance rhetoricians, including no less authorities than Aristotle and Erasmus.[17] Praising the world for what it should be but is not is a form of dispraise. The idealized picture of the world is at once a mirror and a lamp for the actual world it transforms: it sends the reader back to life to see its realities but at the same time directs his way to a radical reformation. Jonson's own recognition of the subversive and ultimately transforming power of poetry of praise accounts for his consistent use of the genre in his lyrics, and his assimilation of the genre into the literary forms he chose to work in, like comedy, tragedy, and most of all, court pageant and masque. And his own understanding of the workings of power accounts for the privileged position of the reader/understander in his poetic program. For him, poetry can reform and transform the world only through the reader who correctly understands the poet's intention. His various devices to secure right—accurate and ethically sound—interpretation are at once a defense against the problematic web of power relations he is caught in and an act of active remaking of it in the shape of his ideals. In that sense, the reader is the vital link between author and text, and between writing and doing. It is only the reader/understander who can find and complete the historical significance the poet intends for his work. The area where the dialectic between history and ideal takes place, the area where fact and fiction meet, is first in the author, next in text, but finally in the reader/understander's understanding and active doing.

What Jonson does in his poetry of praise, then, is not to articulate in so many devious words the dominant ideology of his society, but to reshape the society by commenting upon it, by idealizing its possibilities, and by activating the transforming power of Sidneian poetry in the reader's mind. He shows how the poet can still maintain his independence in and through poetry, how he can still exert real power in shaping himself and his world, which is the poet's way of effecting a true dialectic between fact and fiction, history and ideal.

Notes

Introduction

1. Edmund Wilson, "Morose Ben Jonson," 63–64; Arthur Marotti, "All About Jonson's Poetry," 209; Ian Donaldson, "Jonson and Anger"; John Gordon Sweeney, *Jonson and the Psychology of Public Theater: To Coin the Spirit, Spread the Soul*, 16.

2. O. B. Hardison, *The Enduring Monument: A Study of the Idea of Praise in Renaissance Literary Theory and Practice*; Bernard Weinberg, *A History of Literary Criticism in the Italian Renaissance*; Baxter Hathaway, *The Age of Criticism: The Late Renaissance in Italy*; Brian Vickers, "Epideictic and Epic in the Renaissance."

3. Vickers, "Epideictic and Epic," 513.

Chapter 1: Biography into Poetry

1. Algernon C. Swinburne, *A Study of Ben Jonson*, 107.

2. In the introduction to their edition of Jonson's poems, Herford and Simpson observe that "practically, the whole of these scattered pieces of verse are what are called 'occasional'. They arose directly out of particular events in Jonson's experience, or out of actual relations with friends or foes. . . . They reflect, moreover, this experience and these relations simply and directly, with a minimum of literary elaboration or adornment, and with an eye to immediate practical effect. . . . But these 'occasional' utterances . . . owe almost nothing . . . to invention. . . . the shaping imagination . . . appears all but completely suspended" (*H&S* 2:338). But many other Jonson scholars try to place Jonson's occasional poems in context larger and more general than those of their immediate occasions. O. B. Hardison (in *The Enduring Monument*) emphasizes Jonson's use of Renaissance epideictic rhetoric; George Burke Johnston (in *Ben Jonson: Poet*) explains Jonson's supposed mysogyny as an inheritance from medieval pulpit satire, from which Elizabethan formal verse satirists take the image of woman as an embodiment of vanity and lust (70–95); Hugh Maclean (in "Ben Jonson's Poems: Notes on the Ordered Society"), David Wykes (in "Ben Jonson's 'Chast Booke'—The *Epigrammes*"), and W. H. Herendeen

(in "Like a Circle Bounded in Itself: Jonson, Camden, and the Strategies of Praise") argue that Jonson's poems create a universal moral vision out of the particular events or persons that he celebrates or blames at particular moments of history; and Jonathan Z. Kamholtz (in "Ben Jonson's *Epigrammes* and Poetic Occasions"), stressing the interplay between fact and fiction in Jonson's poems, maintains that Jonson "transforms people into poetic problems; public occasions become, literally, poetic occasions" (78).

3. Percy Simpson's commentary is based on his own article, "Ben Jonson and Cecilia Bulstrode," which treats the possible relationships between the epigram and the epitaph in more detail.

4. For detailed discussions of Jonson's attitudes toward history, see Edward B. Partridge, "Ben Jonson's *Epigrammes:* The Named and the Nameless"; and Richard S. Peterson, *Imitation and Praise in the Poems of Ben Jonson,* 44–61.

5. Biographical details given here are taken from John Donne, *Letters to Severall Persons of Honour (1651),* 215–16; J. A. Harper, "Ben Jonson and Mrs. Bulstrode," 150; Percy Simpson, "Ben Jonson and Cecilia Bulstrode," 187; H&S 1:59, 2:356, 11:87, 130–31; Herbert Grierson, ed., *The Poems of John Donne* 2:212–14; R. C. Bald, *John Donne: A Life,* 177–79; and W. Milgate, ed., *The Epithalamions, Anniversaries and Epicedes,* 182–83. Future references to Donne's poems and letters will be identified by editor, title of edition, and page number.

6. Even speculations about her life are scanty. Relying on Sir Edward Coke's description of her as one "that waits on the Countess of Bedford" and is likely to know well about the goings-on around the court, B. N. De Luna conjectures that Cecilia Bulstrode may have been Robert Cecil's informant in the Gunpowder Plot, in which Jonson and Sir John Roe, the author of the "Elegie to Mris Boulstred: 1602" ("Shall I goe force an Elegie?"), played "mysterious roles of some sort," and traces reflections of her image in Fulvia of *Catiline* and Celia of *Volpone (Jonson's Romish Plot: A Study of "Catiline" and its Historical Context,* 156–69). In an undated letter to George Gerrard, Donne says "I came from thence [London] upon *Thursday,* where I left Sir Tho. Roe so indulgent to his sorrow, as it had been an injury to have interrupted it with my unuseful company. I have done nothing of that kinde as your Letter intimates, in the memory of that good Gentlewoman" (*Letters,* 39). Bald and Milgate agree that the remark suggests Cecilia Bulstrode was Sir Thomas Roe's lover at the time of her death. But there is no evidence that the "good Gentlewoman" is indeed Cecilia Bulstrode, except what one can infer from the fact that it was Gerrard that requested Ben Jonson to write some verses on her death. See Bald, *John Donne: A Life,* 177; Milgate, ed., *The Epithalamions,* 183.

7. The two erotic elegies, which Grierson ascribes to Sir John Roe, are collected as Donne's in some manuscripts (Grierson, ed., *Poems* 2:cxxix–cxxxv). For the elegies themselves, see Grierson, ed., *Poems* 1:412, 410. For Donne's elegies, see Milgate, ed., *The Epithalamions,* 59–63. The authorship of the elegy "Death be not proud" (Grierson, ed., *Poems* 1:422) is also uncertain. It was first printed in 1635 as Donne's. Grierson attributes it to the Countess of Bedford, suggesting that it might have been written as a reply to Donne's "Elegie on Mris Boulstred" ("Death I recant"; see Grierson, ed., *Poems* 2:cxliii–cxlv). Bald (*John Donne: A Life,* 179) and Milgate, ed., (*The Epithalamions,* 235–37) concur. For Edward, Lord Herbert of Cherbury's poem, see *The Poems English and Latin of Edward, Lord Herbert of Cherbury,* ed. G. C. Moore Smith, 20–21.

8. *The Rhetoric of Aristotle,* trans. Lane Cooper, 1.9/1368a35.

9. Jack D. Winner (in "Ben Jonson's *Epigrammes* and the Conventions of Formal Verse Satire") argues that Jonson includes epigrams of praise in *Epigrammes* to

provide the "value center" for satiric epigrams, and by that means to depart from the other Elizabethan formal verse satirists, whose intemperate and indiscriminate satirical attacks fail to present to the reader a comprehensive vision of the world.

10. A number of scholars have discussed this aspect of Jonson's use of names in his epigrams of praise and blame. See, for example, Wykes, "Ben Jonson's 'Chast Booke'"; Partridge, "Ben Jonson's *Epigrammes*"; Harris Friedberg, "Ben Jonson's Poetry: Pastoral, Georgic, Epigram"; Judith Gardiner, *Craftsmanship in Context;* and Herendeen, "Like a Circle Bounded in Itself," which includes an excellent discussion on the significance of the act of naming in Jonson as an act of confirmation of the moral qualities inherent in people.

11. The terms *stylization* and *idealization* used in this chapter to describe Jonson's treatment of the actual person Cecilia Bulstrode *become* almost interchangeable in the course of discussion, because his major method of idealization *is* stylization. But the contexts should make clear that *stylization* emphasizes formal aspects of the treatment, *idealization* its ethical and conceptual aspects.

12. For a discussion of Jonson's use of prostitution as an analogy for "a debased, parodic form of the ideal contract between a writer and his reader," see Jennifer Brady, "'Beware the Poet': Authority and Judgment in Jonson's *Epigrammes*."

13. Donne, for example, expresses his disgust with the court in his satires and personal letters. See "Satyre 4" ("Well; I may now receive, and die"; Grierson, ed., *Poems* 1:158–68); and *Letters,* 12–13, 160.

14. For the interpretation of the epitaph I am much indebted to Francis W. Weitzmann, "Notes on the Elizabethan 'Elegie'"; A. L. Bennett, "The Principal Rhetorical Conventions in the Renaissance Personal Elegy"; and above all, Hardison, *The Enduring Monument.*

15. In his discussion of "Epitaph on Elizabeth, L. H.," Hardison says brevity and restraint are the two most prominent characteristics of a Jonsonian epitaph (*The Enduring Monument,* 124–26). G. W. Pigman III (in "Suppressed Grief in Jonson's Funeral Poetry") traces the intellectual origin of Jonson's suppression of grief in his funeral poetry back to the "rigorism" held by the Church fathers toward death and mourning for the dead.

Chapter 2: *Jonson's Factual Drama*

1. The quotation from Pepys's diary is taken from Herford and Simpson's edition of Ben Jonson (*H&S* 9:241). For the stage history of the two tragedies, see *H&S* 9:190–92, 240–45; and for the stage history of *Catiline* in particular, see Robert Gale Noyes, *Ben Jonson on the English Stage, 1660–1776.*

2. George K. Hunter, "A Roman Thought: Renaissance Attitude to History Exemplified in Shakespeare and Jonson," 108; Robert Ornstein, *The Moral Vision of Jacobean Tragedy,* 103. See also T. S. Eliot, *Essays on Elizabethan Drama;* George A. E. Parfit, "Virtue and Pessimism in Three Plays by Ben Jonson"; Jacob I. DeVilliers, "Ben Jonson's Tragedies"; Jonas Barish's introduction to his edition of *Sejanus;* and for a more recent study, John Gordon Sweeney, *Jonson and the Psychology of Public Theater,* especially chapter 2.

3. Critical opinions on Jonson's extraordinary fidelity to sources in his tragedies are divided into two opposite and complementary camps. Critics like Geoffrey Hill (in "'The World's Proportion': Jonson's Dramatic Poetry in *Sejanus* and *Catiline*") and DeVilliers (in "Ben Jonson's Tragedies") hold that by merely reconstructing history Jonson failed to create tragedies. Joseph Allen Bryant, Jr. (in "The Significance of Ben Jonson's First Requirement for Tragedy: 'Truth of Argument,'" and "*Catiline* and the

Nature of Jonson's Tragic Fable"), Angela G. Dorenkamp (in "Jonson's *Catiline:* History as the Trying Faculty"), and Barish (in the introductory essay to his edition of *Sejanus*) maintain that his historical accuracy is justifiable when one sees *Sejanus* and *Catiline* as dramatized histories.

4. Tacitus, *The Annals of Imperial Rome,* trans. Michael Grant; Sallust, *Conspiracy of Catiline,* trans. S. A. Handford.

5. It is possible to say that in his Roman tragedies Jonson reformulates the epideictic poet's problem into a problem of historical interpretation, impelled by the two competing ideas of history in the Renaissance—the traditional medieval idea of history as a branch of moral philosophy, and an emerging historicism that emphasized the role of particular facts in creating the "spirit" of a particular age. Jonson's idea of history is a characteristically Renaissance amalgamation of the old and the new. In *Underwood* 24, an epigram prefixed to Raleigh's *History of the World* (1614), he describes history in entirely conventional terms, concluding the poem with a translation of Cicero's much repeated definition of history as "testis temporum, lux veritatis, vita memoriae, magistra vitae, nuntia vetustatis" (*De Oratore* 2.9.36). In the poem, as in Cicero's dicta, history is described as performing those epideictic functions Sidney attributes to poetry: it delights and instructs with true examples from the past, rewards the good with immortal fame, and punishes the evil with everlasting infamy. History is a record of timeless exempla. And the historian's task, like that of Sidney's poet, is to vindicate and restore, uncovering some unchanging truth beneath the apparent diversity of particular persons and events. Moving as he did in a circle of "new historians" and antiquarians like William Camden, John Selden, Henry Savile, and Sir Robert Cotton, however, Jonson must have been well aware of the implications of their "historical method," which insisted on faithful reconstruction and analysis of the past on the basis of the verifiable. By emphasizing the importance of particular facts in their own right, this new methodology, in theory, separates history's function from poetry's, and the historical from the poetic interpretation: the historian is allowed to teach only such moral lessons as naked facts of life might be able to without the comforting rhetoric of fiction. In *Sejanus* and *Catiline,* Jonson attempts to reconcile the two ideas of history and by that means recombine history and poetry, giving fact a poetic form and conferring on fiction the authority of fact. The new empirical attitude is reflected in his unprecedented fidelity to sources and his attention to the total contexts of particular events, while the old identification of history and poetry is maintained in the use of history as poetic material and above all in the moral vision and self-reflexiveness that make the two tragico-histories so characteristically Jonsonian.

For detailed studies of Jonson's handling of historical sources, see Barish's introduction to his edition of *Sejanus,* and the introduction and "Appendix B: Jonson's Classical Sources" of W. F. Bolton and Jane F. Gardner's Regents' Renaissance Drama edition of *Catiline.* In "The Nature of Jonson's Roman History," not available to me at the time of writing this chapter, Philip J. Ayers provides a detailed examination of changes Jonson has made on the history of the period covered in *Sejanus* and *Catiline.* He concludes that Jonson offers not a historian's interpretation of the period but a poet's highly stylized account of it. Jonson uses the history of Sejanus's and Catiline's time as an illustration of the moral system he espouses. Hence the stark contrasts between the vicious and the virtuous characters in the two Roman histories. Although Ayers's examination supports my point here, it does not explain why Jonson chooses to use those historical facts when he could just as well invent a moral exemplum of his own. That he uses the period as a moral rather than political exemplum does not necessarily mean that he lacks historical consciousness. It is more likely that he has not yet overcome the limited historicism of the previous age, which he shares with Raleigh among many others. For ideas of history in the Renaissance, see F. J. Levy, *Tudor Historical Thought;* Herschel Baker, *The Race of Time: Three Lectures on Renaissance Historiography;* Lawrence Manley, *Convention, 1500–1750; and Kevin Sharpe, Sir Robert Cotton 1586–1631: History and Politics in Early Modern England.*

6. In his "Self-Reflexive Art of Ben Jonson's *Sejanus,*" Arthur F. Marotti examines the pervasiveness of self-reflexive rhetoric and the playacting and play making in *Sejanus.* But he reaches much the same conclusion as critics like Ornstein reach: "The problem with *Sejanus,* as I have suggested, is that Jonson overdoes the theater metaphor and the self-consciousness of the artifice. Instead of believing that characters make relatively free decisions in a world in which freedom is possible, the audience sees their freedom as either a negative thing (Silius's freedom to die) or, as Barish suggests, an illusion. Such a world resists the spiritual and emotional release tragedy should offer" (218). The problem of this kind of evaluation is that it is based on preconceived assumptions about tragedy and measures any given play against those assumptions. Such an approach is patently inadequate to explain a writer like Jonson, who habitually modifies the received conventions of traditional genres. The closed world of the play that Marotti depreciates is a meaningful element in *Sejanus,* a play that explores the sinister resemblances between tyranny and authorial control over dramatic characters.

7. That Jonson's tragedies share with his comedies the same concern about the ambiguous nature of poetic creation has been variously noted by Alvin Kernan, in his introduction to his Yale edition of *The Alchemist,* and Alexander Leggatt, in *Ben Jonson: His Vision and His Art.* In *Ben Jonson, Dramatist,* Anne Barton finds a more fundamental affinity between Jonsonian tragedy and comedy: she argues that *Sejanus* and *Cataline* show a "persistent, and sometimes disruptive, inclination toward comedy" (156). Jonson often blurs conventional distinctions between comedy and tragedy in his search for a medium appropriate for his vision of life.

8. In *James I and the Politics of Literature: Shakespeare, Donne, and Their Contemporaries,* Jonathan Goldberg argues that there is an indissoluble relationship between power and theater, or in his own words, "the staging of power and the powers of the stage" (166). He maintains that "the Roman plays that came to claim the stage in the Jacobean period reflect the style of the monarch and James's sense of himself as royal actor. . . . In the Roman heroes, the Jacobean stage offers the image of the tragedy implicit in the royal role of the actor replaying the spectral kingdom of Augustus on the stage of history. . . . Monarchs and dramatists speak the same language, pursue the same concerns: the nature of conscience, the relation between inner states and external ones, private lives and public persons, absolutist identity and recreative role playing" (165–66). The applicability of this theory to the particular play *Sejanus,* he says, must be evident from the fact that the comparison between James I and Tiberius had some currency at the time of its performance. While I do not disagree with him about the relationship between power and theater, I want to emphasize that the analogy between king and poet includes the possibility that the poet can participate in the king's exercise of political power. Jonson envisions in *Discoveries* an actively reciprocal relationship between the king and the poet: "Learning needs rest: Sovereignty gives it. Sovereignty needs counsell: Learning affords it" (*H&S* 8:65–66). The two are bound to each other through mutual creation and reflection; they share the authorship of the golden world, since the king, and no one else, has the political power to translate the poet's golden fiction into reality. For attempts to read the two tragedies as "political tragedies" influenced by Machiavelli,

see Ornstein, *The Moral Vision of Jacobean Tragedy;* Michael J. C. Echuero, "The Conscience of Politics and Jonson's *Catiline*"; K. M. Burton, "The Political Tragedies of Chapman and Ben Jonson"; and Daniel C. Boughner, "Sejanus and Machiavelli." For discussions of the Renaissance comparison between state and theater, see Anne Righter [Barton], *Shakespeare and the Idea of Play;* and Leonard F. Dean. "*Richard II:* The State and the Image of the Theater." See also my chapter 4.

9. For an excellent discussion of the close alliance between tyranny and misinterpretation, see George E. Rowe, Jr., "Ben Jonson's Quarrel with Audience and Its Renaissance Context." See also my chapter 5.

10. In *Radical Tragedy: Religion, Ideology, and Power in the Drama of Shakespeare and His Contemporaries,* Jonathan Dollimore argues that the political radicalism of *Sejanus* is to be found in its "historical realism," its demystification of the idea of political power as fate (134–38).

11. W. F. Bolton and Jane F. Gardner's introduction to their edition of *Catiline*, xii.

12. Thomas Greene, "Ben Jonson and the Centered Self."

Chapter 3: Fact and Fiction

1. Jonson professes similar ideas in his prefaces and addresses to the reader. In the second prologue to *Epicoene or The Silent Woman,* for example, he summarizes the doctrine in the same terms: "*Poet* never credit gain'd / By writing truths, but things (like truths) well fain'd" (*H&S* 5:164.9–10).

2. See the address "To the Readers" prefixed to *Sejanus* (*H&S* 4:350–51). Bryant, in "Ben Jonson's First Requirement for Tragedy," finds a link between Jonson's idea of history and his advocacy of the historically verifiable as the object of mimesis: Jonson conceives of history as a branch of moral philosophy that delights and instructs with true examples of the past. In *Sejanus* and *Catiline,* Bryant argues, Jonson tries to import history into poetry. See my chapter 2, especially note 5. For discussions of Tudor historiography and its interaction with poetry, see Baker, *The Race of Time;* Levy, *Tudor Historical Thought;* and Louis B. Wright, "The Elizabethan Middle-Class Taste for History."

3. Arthur Marotti's distinction of the "Apollonian" and the "Dionysian" sides of Jonson ("All About Jonson's Poetry") is useful in understanding Jonson's divided loyalties to two different ideas of poetry. Marotti observes that the genesis of Jonson's art is not in his "Horatian pose of sanity and moderation" but in his urge to vent and transform his "Dionysian" private vision into "Apollonian" forms of art (210). This explains in part his profound concern with gaps between facts and the fictions he has made of those facts. The greater the gaps are, the more insistent his protestations of the factuality of his fictions become.

4. For an examination of the mirror image in this poem as an expression for the mutually reflective relationship between text, reader, and poet, see William E. Cain, "Mirrors, Intentions, and Texts in Ben Jonson."

5. Wesley Trimpi, *Ben Jonson's Poems: A Study of the Plain Style,* 191–238.

6. William E. Cain, "The Place of the Poet in Jonson's 'To Penshurst' and 'To My Muse,'" 47.

7. Erasmus, *Opus Epistolarum Erasmi,* ed. P. S. Allen, 1:397, quoted in Barbara Kiefer Lewalski, *Donne's "Anniversaries" and the Poetry of Praise: The Creation of a Symbolic Mode,* 18. In *Dryden and the Tradition of Panegyric,* describing the panegyric tradition in the Renaissance, James D. Garrison distinguishes two themes (of

"restoration" and "limitation") and two audiences (of "the king" and "the people") of panegyric narrowly defined as *laus regis* (61–63).

8. William Nelson, *Fact or Fiction: The Dilemma of the Renaissance Storyteller,* 114. Hathaway, in *The Age of Criticism,* recognizes the same attitude in Italian Renaissance literary theorists: most of those who emphasized the factuality of poetic imitation "accepted a naive position that truth belongs certainly to the domain of actual particular fact and only dubiously does it apply to rational constructs" (161). Indeed, much of the effort to justify imaginative literature, or poetic fiction, was devoted to answering the charge that fiction is a lie and the poet a liar. See Hathaway, *The Age of Criticism,* 159–66; Joel Elias Spingarn, *A History of Literary Criticism in the Renaissance,* 3–23; and Weinberg, *A History of Literary Criticism in the Italian Renaissance,* 669–71.

9. See Nelson's *Fact or Fiction;* and Barish's introduction to the Yale *Sejanus.* In real life, Sidney was well aware of the moral and political utility of history. Indeed, he was a historian of a sort himself under the guidance of Hubert Languet. For a discussion of Sidney's idea of history, see Elizabeth Story Donno, "Old Mouse-eaten Records: History in Sidney's *Apology*"; and F. J. Levy, "Sir Philip Sidney and the Idea of History."

10. Hardison, *The Enduring Monument,* 43–60. Brian Vickers, on the other hand, in his "Epideictic and Epic," describes the problem as a consequence of the Renaissance dismissal of the factual representation as inferior to the poetic: "Plato's acceptance of epideictic depended on its being true, praising gods or men who deserved to be praised, and one of the defenses of panegyric has always been that it was based on fact. Yet fact was now the province of history, and the fiction of poetry was often confused by its opponent as lies. How to reconcile the supposedly factual content of epideictic with its poetic of fictive mode was a problem not all Renaissance theorists solved" (513). See also my introduction.

11. In 1597, Jonson was imprisoned for his share in the lost comedy *The Isle of Dogs,* which had been denounced to the Privy Council as a "lewd plai," containing "very seditious & sclandrous matter" (*H&S* 1:217–18). For *Sejanus,* performed in 1603, Jonson was cited before the Privy Council on charges of treason (*H&S* 1:36–37). And in 1604, Jonson voluntarily imprisoned himself for his share in *Eastward Ho,* which contained some satire on the Scots, including a caricature of James I himself (*H&S* 1:38).

12. Hardison, *The Enduring Monument,* 54, 56.

13. Because *pictura* is a verbal picture, its use as a device to unite the actual and the ideal, the particular and the generic, can be compared to that of Renaissance *impresses* and hieroglyphs, which were profoundly literary. They externalize particular qualities of a particular person, according to D. J. Gordon in his "Roles and Mysteries," but establish at the same time a "role," representative of persons in similar conditions, "capable of being related to a body of relevant abstractions" (18).

14. Raymond Williams, *The Country and the City,* 30.

15. In "The Place of the Poet," Cain argues that "To Penshurst" is not simply a "mystification" of an economic system, as William takes the poem to be. It betrays "the poet's ambivalent feelings" toward the system and his own place as a poet-praiser in it, especially through a tactic of negation. By enumerating the things that Penshurst is not, Jonson praises the economic system of the Penshurst community but at the same time reveals its less idealistic aspects. Cain's suggestion that this idealistic poem records Jonson's realistic perception of the negative sides of Penshurst is similar in substance to Don E. Wayne's more recent assertion of the poem's subversive

potential. In his *Penshurst: The Semiotics of Place and the Poetics of History,* Wayne argues that the text of the poem registers social contradictions in Jacobean England in a way that "enables alternative forms of praxis in the wider social sphere to be perceived as possible" (130).

16. Lewalski, *Donne's "Anniversaries" and the Poetry of Praise,* 36.

17. Ibid., 46.

18. J. B. Leishman, "Shakespeare's 'un-Platonic Hyperbole," in *Themes and Variations on Shakespeare's Sonnets,* 163.

19. In Sonnet 17, Shakespeare says that posterity might think his praise of his friend mere hyperbole. But this concern itself is used as a form of praise, a strategy to persuade the friend of the need to procreate, and an expression of his love of his friend.

20. For a detailed account of Sir Robert Sidney's domestic affairs, see J. C. A. Rathmell, "Jonson, Lord Lisle, and Penshurst." For information on Egerton's life, consult the *Dictionary of National Biography.*

21. Richard C. Newton, " 'Ben./Jonson': The Poet in the Poems."

22. Jonson said to Drummond that Shakespeare wanted art (*Conversations H&S* 1:133.50). And in *Discoveries* he proclaimed that Shakespeare should have blotted a thousand lines (*H&S* 8:538).

Chapter 4: Jonson's Meta-Masques

1. Francis Bacon, Essay 37, "Of Masques and Triumphs," *Essays;* Samuel Daniel, *The Vision of the Twelve Goddess,* ed. Joan Rees, in *A Book of Masques in Honour of Allardyce Nicoll,* ed. T. J. B. Spencer and Stanley Wells, 25. Modern criticism of the Jacobean and Caroline masque in fact began as an effort to rescue the genre from this Baconian stigma that it was a mere toy, or a gross flattery. Such effort was first begun by Enid Welsford (in *The Court Masque*), Ernest William Talbert (in "The Interpretation of Jonson's Courtly Spectacles"), and Allan H. Gilbert (in *The Symbolic Persons in the Masques of Ben Jonson*), who found in the genre a mirror for magistrates; the work was carried on by Dolora Cunningham (in "The Jonsonian Masque as a Literary Form"), W. Todd Furniss (in "Ben Jonson's Masques"), Stephen Orgel (in *The Jonsonian Masque*), and John C. Meagher (in *Method and Meaning in Jonson's Masques*). In 1968, deploring what she considered these critics' formalistic bias, Inga-Stina Ewbank found the "final prospect" of evaluative masque criticism "gloomy" (" 'The Eloquence of Masques': A Retrospective View of Masque Criticism. A Review Article," 327). Her gloomy prognostication was based on the fact that the masque as a form of *Gesamtkunst* posed an unusually acute problem, because no single approach could take account of all the elements that went into the making of a masque. Since then, the focus of critical attention has shifted from how to evaluate "the absolute worth of one masque over another" to how to see the masque in its total social and political context. This change in direction has gathered extra momentum from a recent tendency in Anglo-American literary scholarship to read a literary text primarily as a product of the society in which it was born and to which it gave shape. For some scholars of English Renaissance courtly culture, the masque has become a meta-text *par excellence*. The distance that masque criticism has traveled in less than two decades can be measured by comparing Stephen Orgel's *Jonsonian Masque* (1965) with his *Illusion of Power: Political Theater in the English Renaissance* (1975). The earlier book's formalist concern to show how Jonson created a well-wrought poem of a masque by integrating discrete elements into a coherent whole is

replaced in the later book by an examination of the masque's role in Jacobean and Caroline power politics and ideological warfare. The tendency to read the genre in its social context also characterizes the 1977 issue of *Renaissance Drama* on "The Celebratory Mode." A still more recent expression of that tendency is the 1983 special issue of *New Literary History* on new interpretations of the Renaissance. One essay collected in this issue, which examines the "courtliness" of the Renaissance, characterizes the masque as "the quintessence of a courtly text" (Heinrich Plett, "Aesthetic Constituents in the Courtly Culture of Renaissance England," 614). Louis Adrian Montrose, in "Of Gentlemen and Shepherds: The Politics of Elizabethan Pastoral Form," examines the politics of the Elizabethan pageants and masques as pastorals. Leah Sinanoglou Marcus, in her articles on topicality in Jonson's masques, examines specific textual evidences that substantiate their political origin and significance: see her " 'Present Occasions' and the Shaping of Ben Jonson's Masques"; "The Occasion of Ben Jonson's *Pleasure Reconciled to Virtue*"; and "Masquing Occasions and Masque Structure." David Lindley's recent collection of essays, *The Court Masque*, on the other hand, seems to modify the tendency by linking the social context of the masque to its textual context.

2. For a thorough examination of how "present occasions" of particular marriages can contain "more remov'd *mysteries*," see D. J. Gordon's "*Hymenaei*: Ben Jonson's Masque of Union," and "Ben Jonson's 'Haddington Masque': The Story and the Fable."

3. George Chapman, *The Plays and Poems of George Chapman*, ed. T. M. Parrott, 2:444.

4. See Marcus's "The Occasion." Dale B. J. Randall, *Jonson's Gypsies Unmasked: Background and Theme of "The Gypsies Metamorphosed"*.

5. For studies on the theatrical illusionism in the Stuart court theater, see Allardyce Nicoll, *Stuart Masques and the Renaissance Stage;* Orgel, *Illusion of Power;* and Stephen Orgel and Roy Strong, *Inigo Jones: The Theater of the Stuart Court.* Jonson's reaction to theatricality itself is brilliantly charted by Jonas A. Barish in his "Jonson and the Loathed Stage," chapter 5 of *The Antitheatrical Prejudice*.

6. For the theoretical background of the feud between Jonson and Jones, see D. J. Gordon's classic essay "Poet and Architect: The Intellectual Setting of the Quarrel Between Ben Jonson and Inigo Jones."

7. Samuel Daniel, *Tethys' Festival*, ed. Alexander B. Grosart, 320–21.

8. C. V. Wedgwood's "Last Masque" in *Truth and Opinion* is perhaps the most eloquent reconstruction of this process of changing fiction into fact. Orgel's *Illusion of Power* treats the same subject.

9. Percy Bysshe Shelley, *Charles the First*, in *Poems*, vol. 4 of *The Complete Works*, ed. Roger Ingpen and Walter E. Peck. For an illuminating commentary on the play and the genre of masque, see David Norbrook, "The Reformation of the Masque," in *The Court Masque*, ed. David Lindley, 94–110.

10. Norbrook, "Reformation of the Masque," 95–96.

11. Despites its centrality in understanding Jonson's masques as well as the play itself, the masque in *Cynthia's Revels* has received little attention from critics of Jonsonian masques except as an illustration of the masque's generic function as *laus regis* (as in Gilbert's *Symbolic Persons*). L. A. Beaurline's reading of the play as a whole comes closer to my argument here. In his *Jonson and the Elizabethan Comedy: Essays in Dramatic Rhetoric*, he observes that "two contrasting forces operate in the play, one moving toward a contemplation of an exalted ideal, love of almost unearthly perfection, the other force attacking self-love, showing up the triviality and

pretense of sophisticated life. In the end the first force draws the second into the field, reconciling self-love to its subordinate place" (121). That explains in part Crites' unconventional use of the celebratory genre as a satire against court.

12. Beaurline, in *Jonson and the Elizabethan Comedy,* aptly describes Crites' masque as "a penitential cure that mixes ceremony and satire" (130), suggesting at the same time that the curative power of Crites' masque comes from the moral influence that Cynthia as the bearer of the Platonic high ideal exerts on the vicious.

13. Ibid., 129.

14. For a most illuminating study of this masque, see Jonas A. Barish, *Ben Jonson and the Language of Prose Comedy,* especially chapter 6. See also Jeffrey Fisher, "Love Restored: A Defense of Masquing."

15. The extravagance of the Stuart court spectacle almost justifies Plutus's attack. For detailed accounts, see John Nichols, *The Progresses of James the First;* and G. P. V. Akrigg, *Jacobean Pageant or the Court of King James I.* For a typical Puritan reaction, see William Prynne's *Histrio-Mastix* (1633).

16. In "The Alchemy in Jonson's *Mercury Vindicated,*" Edgar Hill Duncan notes that Jonson uses the literature of alchemy current in his day more extensively in this masque than in *The Alchemist* written five years earlier. From this literature, according to Duncan, Jonson derives the basic ideas of his antimasque—the decaying Nature and the alchemists' "artificial" generation, among others. *The Alchemist,* I think, is the best commentary on the masque and its use of alchemy as a metaphor for the art of poetry. Both the play and the masque distinguish two kinds of alchemy and aspiration to control and reform the world, and both arrive at the same conclusion that true art works with, not against, nature.

17. At the very beginning of Beaumont and Fletcher's *Maid's Tragedy,* Strato identifies the masque with its restrictions, giving birth to the most memorable if the most sarcastic definition of the genre to date:

> LISIPPUS. *Strato* thou hast some skill in poetrie, what think'st thou of a maske, will it be well?
> STRATO. As well as maske can be.
> LISIPPUS. As maske can be?
> STRATO. Yes, they must commend their King, and speake in praise of the assembly, blesse the Bride and groome, in person of some God, they'r tied to the rules of flatterie. (1.1.5–11)

Chapter 5: "Rare Poemes Aske Rare Friends"

1. Jonas Barish, *The Antitheatrical Prejudice,* 139; Timothy Murray, "From Foul Sheets to Legitimate Model: Antitheater, Text, Ben Jonson," 662; Richard C. Newton, "Jonson and the (Re-)Invention of the Book," 31.

2. I owe this reading of the passage especially to A. Leigh DeNeef's "Rereading Sidney's *Apology.*" DeNeef goes much further than I do to argue that Sidney's conception of poetry as imitation should be understood in the context of the Protestant calls for individual and societal reform. The principal poetic acts—writing poetry and reading it—are both imitative of the divine act of creation. Thus "false readings metaphorically recapitulate the first such act [the original mistake of Adam] and are potentially reenactments of the Fall" (187), while right readings lead the reader to ethical actions "done in imitation of God's archetypal act of Creation" (190).

3. Margaret W. Ferguson, *Trials of Desire: Renaissance Defenses of Poetry,* 148. In his *Defence of Poetry* (1579), Thomas Lodge expresses much the same opinion

about the reader's role in the right use of poetry's affective power: "to the ignorant eche thinge that is unknowne semes unprofitable, but a wise man can forsee and prayse by proofe. . . . those of judgment can from the same flower suck honey with the bee, from whence the spider (I mean the ignorant) take their poison" (1:79).

4. Jonson's "plain style," which Trimpi has examined in detail, can be explained in the same way: it serves his purpose of establishing a "right" relationship to his reader, with its proverbial effectiveness as a method of communication and persuasion. Its characteristic lucidity and seeming naturalness help to convince the reader of the accuracy, candor, sincerity, and judgment of the poet in his description and analysis of the real world. For Jonson's concern about misreading, see Rowe's "Ben Jonson's Quarrel."

5. This aspect of Jonson's art has been recognized. For example, in his "Self and Others in Two Poems by Ben Jonson," William E. Cain observes that "one of Jonson's limitations, in fact, is that while he writes in many different genres, he pursues a narrow range of themes: he repeats himself" (167). He argues that Jonson's self-repetition attests "his urge more to clarify than to complicate" and "his desire to polarize experience and make it (to borrow Peter Brook's phrase about 'melodramatic imagination') 'morally legible,' with its good and evil camps sharply differentiated" (168). Cain's psychoanalytic approach complements my more formalist examination of how and why Jonson uses repetition as a strategic defense against misinterpretation.

6. James Howell was able to understand Jonson's "Roman infirmity," the excessive love of one's "brain's issues." See *H&S* 11:420. Of course, Jonson is not alone in his mistrust of the reader. Renaissance addresses to "the Reader" range from somewhat helpless pleadings to the reader not to misuse the poem (as in Gascoign's introductory epistles to *The Poesie*) to stiff-necked directives about how to treat the poem (as in Jonson's epistles to the readers). Renaissance attitudes toward the reader or the audience are not uniform: Jonson's potential destroyer of the poem is as different from Shakespeare's kind and "mending" audience as it is from Sidney's childish reader, whom the poet should cajole into swallowing the "cherry medicine" of the poem.

7. Interestingly enough, Jonson's contemporary commentators seem to have caught the accent of Jonson's directives to the reader and regularly echo his own words. Nathan Field, for example, ends his poem written on the occasion of the publication of *Volpone* in 1605 with, "But, thou that wouldst ore his true praises looke, / First, pray to understand, then read his booke" (*H&S* 11:323.39–40).

8. Liane Norman, "Risk and Redundancy," 286, 287, 291.

9. The significance of naming is perhaps the most widely discussed aspect of Jonson's *Epigrammes*. But the behavior of *name* as a single word in the *Epigrammes* deserves more critical attention than it has received. For discussions on Jonson's naming device, see, for example, Wykes's "Ben Jonson's 'Chast Booke' "; Partridge's "Ben Jonson's *Epigrammes*"; Friedberg's "Ben Jonson's Poetry"; Gardiner's *Craftsmanship in Context*; and Herendeen's "Like a Circle Bounded in Itself."

10. Actual persons addressed more than once are King James (Epigrams 4, 5, 35, 36, 51); John Donne (23, 96); Sir John Roe (27, 32, 33); Robert, Earl of Salisbury (43, 63, 64, 65); Thomas Roe (98, 99); Lucy, Countess of Bedford (76, 84, 94); Sir Henry Goodyer (85, 86); Mary, Lady Worth (103, 105); Clement Edmondes (110, 111); Benjamin Rudyerd (121, 122, 123); William Roe (70, 128); and Alphonso Ferrabosco (130, 131). Vicious types treated more than once are Sir Cod (Epigrams 19, 20, 50); Person Guilty (30, 38); Sir Voluptuous Beast (25, 26); Cheverel (37, 54); Sir Luckless Woo-All (46, 47); Playwright (49, 68, 100); and Courtling (52, 72).

11. *The Rhetoric of Aristotle*, 1.2./1356a.

12. Following Edmund Wilson's lead, many critics of Jonson have "explained" that his insistence on authorial intention as the right meaning of a literary text shows his authoritarian attitude toward the audience. Such an explanation tends to minimize the significance of authorial intention as an integral part of his poetic scheme. But in "Mirrors, Intentions, and Texts," Cain recognizes that in Jonson the relationship between author, text, and reader is indissoluble. He rightly suggests that "Jonson argues that the best reader will recognize ('eye directly') the intention of the author in writing a text. Jonson believes that readers are responsible . . . to the author, and must, if their judgment is to be legitimate, understand his intended meaning. A bad reader is one who misses the author's intended meaning entirely, or else fails to appreciate the good intentions" (17).

13. In "Authors-Readers: Jonson's Community of the Same," Stanley Fish makes the same kind of observation, but in a different context and with a different emphasis. He argues that Jonson resolves or at least bypasses ethical and epistemological dilemmas of representation in the notion of an "author-reader." Assuming a reader whose mind is no different from his own, Jonson substitutes representation with declarations of its needlessness and impossibility (132–47). But my emphasis is here on the smallness of the kind of interpretive community that Jonson envisions. Jonson's search for an ideal reader, who does not need his words in order to understand him, is a project of enlarging his soul into a wide world, which often becomes in effect a project of contracting the wide world into the little room of his own mind. As Cain suggests in "Self and Others," a search for such an ideal reader occurs in Jonson simultaneously with detachment from the world. His public address in the "Epistle answering" and other poems, for example, "takes a characteristic turn: the poet moves away from his reader and instead presents, examines, and communes with himself" (173).

14. Jonson's trust in John Selden was not misplaced: in the preface to his *Titles of Honor* (1614), Selden speaks of "my beloved friend that singular poet M. *Ben: Jonson,* whose speciall Worth in Literature, accurat Judgment, and Performance, known only to that *Few* which are truly able to know him, hath had from me, ever since I began to learn, an increasing admiration" (*H&S* 2:383–84).

Conclusion

1. See Felperin, *Beyond Deconstruction: The Uses and Abuses of Literary Theory,* especially 165–75. For a recent discussion of *ut pictura poesis,* see Henryk Markiewicz, "Ut Pictura Poesis . . . a History of the Topos and the Problem."

2. O. B. Hardison, *The Enduring Monument;* and Brian Vickers, "Epideictic and Epic"; and see also W. R. Johnson, *The Idea of Lyric: Lyric Modes in Ancient and Modern Poetry.*

3. Stephen Greenblatt, *Renaissance Self-Fashioning: From More to Shakespeare,* 257. In his programmatic introduction to a collection of essays he edited, *The Power of Forms in the English Renaissance,* Greenblatt identifies as "new historicism," or "the poetics of culture," the recent attempt to resituate literary texts of the Renaissance among other forms of writing and in relation to "the complex network of institutions, practices, and beliefs that constitute the culture as a whole" (3–6). But the necessity to find an access to Renaissance literature beyond that afforded by either reductive formalism or so-called old historicism and the course such an attempt might take were outlined as early as 1969 by Robert Weimann in his eminently sane essay "Past Significance and Present Meaning in Literary History," which appeared in the

inaugural issue of *New Literary History*. In his more recent contribution to the discussion, "Text and History: Epilogue, 1984," Weimann criticizes Derrida's textualization of history and argues specifically for a historicization of the text through the acts of writing and reading.

Other scholars prominently engaged in revisionist rereading of Renaissance literature are Louis Montrose, Jonathan Goldberg, Arthur Marotti, Annabel Patterson, Don E. Wayne, Alan Sinfield, Leonard Tennehouse, and Jonathan Dollimore. There are of course many others, but I have included in this essay only those who discuss Jonson's work as one of the major texts to be reread. The Winter 1986 issue of *English Literary Renaissance* prints two helpful overviews of the new historicist enterprise, Louis Montrose's "Renaissance Literary Studies and the Subject of History" (5–12), and Jean E. Howard's "The New Historicism in Renaissance Studies" (13–43). I am sympathetic to the new historicist attempt to reread a literary text in its particular contexts, but I have serious reservations about their skeptical view of human activities in general, their preoccupation with the social aspects of a text at the expense of the poet and the poem, their privileging of the theorist-critic as the decoder of the unconsciousness of a text which is not available to "the reader," and the ultimate—and in this case, I think, vicious—hermeneutic circle built into their theory of language and culture that turns all texts into histories, and all histories into texts.

4. Goldberg, *James I and the Politics of Literature*, 220, 225, 230.

5. It should be noted that Goldberg's Jonson is near kin to Greenblatt's Marlowe in their contained rebellions. But criticisms of the reductiveness of this "subversion/containment" paradigm are beginning to be heard among new historicists themselves. Even Greenblatt attempts to explain the text's "subversion" more fully in his "Invisible Bullets: Renaissance Authority and Its Subversion." In *Penshurst*, a book-length explication of "To Penshurst," Wayne argues that the text has the potentiality to reveal social contradictions in a way "that enables alternative forms of praxis in the wider social sphere to be perceived as possible" (130). But the chief contestant is Alan Sinfield, a "cultural materialist" rather than a "new historicist." In his "Power and Ideology: An Outline Theory and Sidney's *Arcadia*," he challenges the paradigm and proposes instead a "contestation" model. He argues, in regard to Sidney, that it is possible to "envisage the literary text not necessarily as subversive, but as a site of contest," and that "the role of the writer as writer is likely to stimulate awareness of the importance of ideological production in the sustaining, negotiating and contesting of power in the state" (274). Montrose, in his *English Literary Renaissance* overview essay, also emphasizes the "*relative* autonomy of specific discourses and their capacity to impact upon the social formation, to make things happen by shaping the consciousness of social beings" (8). See also Dollimore's *Radical Tragedy*, and his introduction to *Political Shakespeare: New Essays in Cultural Materialism*, ed. Jonathan Dollimore and Alan Sinfield. But to my mind these critics do not really go far from the original Greenblatt paradigm. They open the issue of autonomy only so far as to allow the writer the power to assist in constructing a new ideologeme. They retain the initial assumption of power as the only human desideratum. For a brilliant critique of this aspect of new historicism, see also Edward Pechter, "The New Historicism and Its Discontents: Politicizing Renaissance Drama."

6. Goldberg, *James I and the Politics of Literature*, 226.

7. Wayne presents a different view in his *Penshurst*. He argues that the poem, like the house, contains two different ideologies. The one is the conservative one of birth and "house" that sustained the past order; the other belongs to the bourgeois ideology of merit and "home" dominant in the modern age.

8. Arthur Marotti, "John Donne and the Rewards of Patronage," in *The Pa-*

tronage in the Renaissance, ed. Guy Fitch Lytle and Stephen Orgel, 207, 225. See also his essay " 'Love Is Not Love': Elizabethan Sonnet Sequences and the Social Order"; and his recent book *John Donne, Coterie Poet.*

9. Robert C. Evans, " 'Men that are Safe, and Sure': Jonson's 'Tribe of Ben' Epistle in its Patronage Context."

10. Marotti, " 'Love Is Not Love,' " 418.

11. In " 'The Comedians' Liberty': Censorship of the Jacobean Stage Reconsidered," Philip Finkelpearl argues that censorship was much less stricly enforced by James I or his government officials than has been supposed. The government estimated the political power of poets at a much lower rate, regarding them more likely as licensed fools (123–38).

12. Patterson, *Censorship and Interpretation,* 13. Patterson is not alone in her attempt to historicize (and politicize) lyric poetry, a genre dear to New Critics. Lauro Martines's *Society and History in English Renaissance Verse,* articles collected by Chaviva Hŏsek and Patricia Parker in *Lyric Poetry: Beyond New Criticism,* and those collected by Richard Machin and Christopher Norris in *Post-Structuralist Readings of English Poetry,* for example, take part in the enterprise.

13. Patterson, *Censorship and Interpretation,* 120–43.

14. In his recent book *Ben Jonson,* Peter Womack presents a more flexible view of the relationship between Jonson's work and the Jacobean state than that put forward by the new historicists. He argues that the monologic *court word* in Jonson's plays became dialogized in public theaters, because of the heterogeneous audience (76–107).

15. For biographies of Jonson, see *H&S* 1 and 2; Rosalind Miles's *Ben Jonson: His Life and Work.*

16. Topicality, for obvious reasons, has been a focal point in many new-historical discussions of Renaissance literary texts. In a series of articles, Leah Marcus demonstrates the topicality of Jonson's masques: see especially her " 'Present Occasions.' " In *Poetry and Politics in the English Renaissance,* David Norbrook attempts to demonstrate that politics determined not only the content but the rhetoric of Renaissance poetry, instancing numerous topical allusions found in the age's poetic texts.

17. See *The Rhetoric of Aristotle,* 1.9/1368a35, and Erasmus's *Opus Epistolarum Erasmi,* 1:397. For modern discussions of this aspect, see Johnson's *The Idea of Lyric,* 74; and Joanne Altieri's *The Theatre of Praise,* 26–29.

Works Cited

Akrigg, G. P. V. *Jacobean Pageant or the Court of King James I.* New York: Atheneum, 1978.

Altieri, Joanne. *The Theatre of Praise.* Cranbury, N.J.: Associated Univ. Press, 1986.

Aristotle, *Rhetoric.* Trans. Lane Cooper. In *The Rhetoric of Aristotle.* Englewood Cliffs, N.J.: Prentice-Hall, 1932.

Ayers, Philip J. "The Nature of Jonson's Roman History." *English Literary Renaissance* 16 (1986): 166–81.

Bacon, Francis. "Of Masques and Triumphs." In *Essays,* 115–18. London: Dent, 1972.

Baker, Herschel. *The Race of Time: Three Lectures on Renaissance Historiography.* Toronto: Univ. of Toronto Press, 1967.

Bald, R. C. *John Donne: A Life.* Oxford: Clarendon, 1970.

Barish, Jonas A. *Ben Jonson and the Language of Prose Comedy.* Cambridge: Harvard Univ. Press, 1960. Especially chap. 6.

——. Introduction to his edition of *Sejanus,* by Ben Jonson. New Haven: Yale Univ. Press, 1965.

——. "Jonson and the Loathed Stage." Chap. 5 of *The Antitheatrical Prejudice.* Berkeley and Los Angeles: Univ. of California Press, 1981.

Barton, Anne. *Ben Jonson, Dramatist.* Cambridge: Cambridge Univ. Press, 1984.

Beaumont, Francis, and John Fletcher. *The Maid's Tragedy.* Ed. Andrew Gurr. Berkeley and Los Angeles: Univ. of California Press, 1969.

Beaurline, L. A. *Johnson and the Elizabethan Comedy: Essays in Dramatic Rhetoric.* San Marino, Calif.: Huntington Library, 1978.

Bennett, A. L. "The Principal Rhetorical Conventions in the Renaissance Personal Elegy." *Studies in Philology* 51 (1954): 107–26.

Boughner, Daniel C. "Juvenal, Horace, and Sejanus." *Modern Language Notes* 75 (1960): 545–51.

——. "Sejanus and Machiavelli." *Studies in English Literature* 1 (1961): 81–100.

Brady, Jennifer. "'Beware the Poet': Authority and Judgment in Jonson's *Epigrammes.*" *Studies in English Literature* 23 (1983): 95–112.

Bryant, Joseph Allen, Jr. "The Significance of Ben Jonson's First Requirement for Tragedy: 'Truth of Argument.'" *Studies in Philology* 49 (1952): 195–213.

——. "*Catiline* and the Nature of Jonson's Tragic Fable." *PMLA* 69 (1954): 265–77.

Burton, K. M. "The Political Tragedies of Chapman and Ben Jonson." *Essays in Criticism* 2 (1952): 397–412.

Cain, William E. "The Place of the Poet in Jonson's 'To Penshurst' and 'To My Muse.'" *Criticism* 21 (1979): 34–48.

——. "Mirrors, Intentions, and Texts in Ben Jonson." *Essays in Literature* 8 (1981): 11–23.

——. "Self and Others in Two Poems by Ben Jonson." *Studies in Philology* 80 (1983): 163–82.

Chapman, George. *The Plays and Poems of George Chapman.* 2 vols. Ed. T. M. Parrott. London, 1910–14.

Cicero. *The Speeches of Cicero.* Trans. Louis E. Lord. Loeb Classical Library. Cambridge: Harvard Univ. Press, 1964.

Cunningham, Dolora. "The Jonsonian Masque as a Literary Form." *ELH* 22 (1955): 108–24.

Daniel, Samuel. *Tethys' Festival.* Ed. Alexander B. Grosart. Vol. 3 of *The Complete Works in Verse and Prose of Samuel Daniel.* London, 1885.

——. *The Vision of the Twelve Goddess.* Ed. Joan Rees. In *A Book of Masques in Honour of Allardyce Nicoll,* ed. T. J. B. Spencer and Stanley Wells. Cambridge: Cambridge Univ. Press, 1967.

De Luna, B. N. *Jonson's Romish Plot: A Study of "Catiline" and its Historical Context.* Oxford: Clarendon, 1967.

Dean, Leonard F. "*Richard II:* The State and the Image of the Theater." *PMLA* 67 (1952): 211–18.

DeNeef, A. Leigh "Rereading Sidney's *Apology.*" *Journal of Medieval and Renaissance Studies* 10 (1980): 155–91.

DeVilliers, Jacob I. "Ben Jonson's Tragedies." *English Studies* 45 (1964): 433–42.

Dio Cassius. *Dio's Roman History.* Vol. 3. Trans. Ernest Cary. Loeb Classical Library. New York: Macmillan, 1914.

Dollimore, Jonathan. *Radical Tragedy: Religion, Ideology and Power in the Drama of Shakespeare and His Contemporaries.* Brighton: Harvester Press, 1984.

——. "Introduction: Shakespeare, Cultural Materialism and the New Historicism." In *Political Shakespeare: New Essays in Cultural Materialism,* ed. Jonathan Dollimore and Alan Sinfield, 2–17. Manchester: Manchester Univ. Press, 1985.

Donaldson, Ian. "Jonson and Anger." In *English Satire and the Satiric Tradition,* ed. Claude Rawson, 56–71. Oxford: Blackwell, 1984.

Donne, John. *The Epithalamions, Anniversaries and Epicedes.* Ed. W. Milgate. Oxford: Clarendon, 1978.

——. *Letters to Severall Persons of Honour (1651).* Facsimile reproduction. Introduction by M. Thomas Hester. Delmar, N.Y.: Scholars' Facsimiles & Reprints, 1977.

——. *The Poems of John Donne.* Ed. Herbert Grierson. London: Oxford Univ. Press, 1912.

Donno, Elizabeth Story. "Old Mouse-eaten Records: History in Sidney's *Apology.*" *Studies in Philology* 72 (1975): 275–98.

Dorenkamp, Angela G. "Jonson's *Catiline:* History as the Trying Faculty." *Studies in Philology* 67 (1970): 210–20.

Duncan, Edgar Hill. "The Alchemy in Jonson's *Mercury Vindicated.*" *Studies in Philology* 39 (1942): 625–37.

Echuero, Michael J. C. "The Conscience of Politics and Jonson's *Catiline.*" *Studies in English Literature* 6 (1966): 341–56.

Eliot, T. S. *Essays on Elizabethan Drama.* New York: Harcourt, 1932.

English Literary Renaissance 16 (1986). Special issue: *Studies in Renaissance Historicism.*

Erasmus. *Opus Epistolarum Erasmi.* Vol. 1. Ed. P. S. Allen. Oxford: Clarendon, 1906.

Evans, Robert C. "'Men that are Safe, and Sure': Jonson's 'Tribe of Ben' Epistle in its Patronage Context." *Renaissance and Reformation* 14 (1985): 235–54.

Ewbank, Inga-Stina. "'The Eloquence of Masques': A Retrospective View of Masque Criticism. A Review Article." *Renaissance Drama,* n.s. 1 (1968): 307–28.

Felperin, Howard. *Beyond Deconstruction: The Uses and Abuses of Literary Theory.* Oxford: Clarendon, 1985.

Ferguson, Margaret W. *Trials of Desire: Renaissance Defenses of Poetry.* New Haven: Yale Univ. Press, 1985.

Finkelpearl, Philip. "'The Comedians' Liberty': Censorship of the Jacobean Stage Reconsidered." *English Literary Renaissance* 16 (1986): 123–38.

Fish, Stanley. "Authors-Readers: Jonson's Community of the Same." In *Lyric Poetry: Beyond New Criticism,* ed. Chaviva Hösek and Patricia Parker. Ithaca: Cornell Univ. Press, 1985.

Fisher, Jeffrey. "*Love Restored:* A Defense of Masquing." In *The Celebratory Mode,* ed. Leonard Barkan, special issue of *Renaissance Drama,* n.s. 8 (1977).

Friedberg, Harris. "Ben Jonson's Poetry: Pastoral, Georgic, Epigram." *English Literary Renaissance* 4 (1974): 111–36.

Furniss, W. Todd. "Ben Jonson's Masques." In *Three Studies in the Renaissance,* 89–179. New Haven: Yale Univ. Press, 1958.

Gardiner, Judith. *Craftsmanship in Context.* The Hague: Mouton, 1975.

Garrison, James D. *Dryden and the Tradition of Panegyric.* Berkeley and Los Angeles: Univ. of California Press, 1975.

Gascoign, George. Introductory epistles to *The Poesie.* In *The Complete Works of George Gascoign.* Ed. John W. Cunliffe. Cambridge: Cambridge Univ. Press, 1907.

Gilberts, Allan H. "The Function of the Masques in the *Cynthia's Revels.*" *Philological Quarterly* 22 (1943): 211–30.

——. *The Symbolic Persons in the Masques of Ben Jonson.* Durham: Univ. of North Carolina Press, 1948.

Goldberg, Jonathan. *James I and the Politics of Literature: Jonson, Shakespeare, Donne, and Their Contemporaries.* Baltimore: Johns Hopkins Univ. Press, 1983.

Gordon, D. J. "*Hymenaei:* Ben Jonson's Masque of Union." *Journal of the Warburg and Courtauld Institutes* 8 (1945): 107–45.

——. "Ben Jonson's 'Haddington Masque': The Story and the Fable." *Modern Language Review* 42 (1947): 180–87.

——. "Poet and Architect: The Intellectual Setting of the Quarrel Between Ben Jonson and Inigo Jones." *Journal of the Warburg and Courtauld Institutes* 12 (1949): 107–45.

——. "Roles and Mysteries." In *The Renaissance Imagination,* ed. Stephen Orgel. Berkeley and Los Angeles: Univ. of California Press, 1975.

Greenblatt, Stephen. *Renaissance Self-Fashioning: From More to Shakespeare.* Chicago: Univ. of Chicago Press, 1980.

——. "Invisible Bullets: Renaissance Authority and Its Subversion." *Glyph* 8 (1981): 40–61.

——. Introduction to *The Power of Forms in the English Renaissance,* ed. Stephen Greenblatt. Norman, Okla.: Pilgrim Books, 1982.

Greene, Thomas M. "Ben Jonson and the Centered Self." *Studies in English* 10 (1970): 325–48.

Hardison, O. B. *The Enduring Monument: A Study of the Idea of Praise in Renaissance Literary Theory and Practice.* Chapel Hill: Univ. of North Carolina Press, 1962.

Harper, J. A. "Ben Jonson and Mrs. Bulstrode." *N&Q* 28 (1863): 150.

Hathaway, Baxter. *The Age of Criticism: The Late Renaissance in Italy.* Westport, Conn.: Greenwood, 1962.

Herbert, Edward. *The Poems English and Latin of Edward, Lord Herbert of Cherbury.* Ed. G. C. Smith. Oxford: Clarendon, 1968.

Herendeen, W. H. "Like a Circle Bounded in Itself: Jonson, Camden, and the Strategies of Praise." *Journal of Medieval and Renaissance Studies* 11 (1981): 137–67.

Hill, Geoffrey. " 'The World's Proportion': Jonson's Dramatic Poetry in *Sejanus* and *Catiline*." In *Jacobean Theater,* ed. J. R. Brown and B. Harris. London: Univ. of London Press, 1960.

Howard, Jean E. "The New Historicism in Renaissance Studies." *English Literary Renaissance* 16 (1986): 13–43.

Hunter, George K. "A Roman Thought: Renaissance Attitude to History Exemplified in Shakespeare and Jonson." In *An English Miscellany Presented to W. S. Mackie,* ed. Brian S. Lee, 93–118. Cape Town: Oxford Univ. Press, 1977.

Johnson, W[alter] R[alph]. *The Idea of Lyric: Lyric Modes in Ancient and Modern Poetry.* Berkeley and Los Angeles: Univ. of California Press, 1982.

Johnston, George Burke. *Ben Jonson: Poet.* New York: Octagon, 1970.

Jonson, Ben. *Ben Jonson.* Ed. C. H. Herford and Percy and Evelyn Simpson. 11 vols. Oxford: Clarendon, 1925–52.

——. *Sejanus.* Ed. Jonas A. Barish. The Yale Ben Jonson. New Haven: Yale Univ. Press, 1965. Especially Barish's introduction.

——. *Catiline.* Ed. W. F. Bolton and Jane F. Gardner. Regents' Renaissance Drama. Lincoln: Univ. of Nebraska Press, 1973.

——. *The Alchemist.* Ed. Alvin Kernan. The Yale Ben Jonson. New Haven: Yale Univ. Press, 1974. Especially Kernan's introduction.

——. *Poems.* Ed. Ian Donaldson. New York: Oxford Univ. Press, 1975.

Kamholtz, Jonathan Z. "Ben Jonson's *Epigrammes* and Poetic Occasions." *Studies in English Literature* 23 (1983): 77–94.

Kernan, Alvin. Introduction to his edition of *The Alchemist,* by Ben Jonson. New Haven: Yale Univ. Press, 1974.

Leggatt, Alexander. *Ben Jonson: His Vision and His Art.* New York: Methuen, 1981.

Leishman, J. B. "Shakespeare's 'un-Platonic Hyperbole.' " In *Themes and Variations on Shakespeare's Sonnets.* London: Hutchinson, 1961.

Levy, F. J. "Sir Philip Sidney and the Idea of History." *Bibliotheque D'Humanisme et Renaissance* 26 (1964): 608–17.

——. *Tudor Historical Thought.* San Marino, Calif.: Huntington Library, 1967.

Lewalski, Barbara Kiefer. *Donne's "Anniversaries" and the Poetry of Praise: The Creation of a Symbolic Mode.* Princeton: Princeton Univ. Press, 1973.

Lindley, David, ed. *The Court Masque.* Manchester: Manchester Univ. Press, 1984.

Lodge, Thomas. *Defence of Poetry.* In vol. 1 of *Elizabethan Critical Essays,* ed. Gregory Smith, 61–68. Oxford: Clarendon, 1904.

Machin, Richard, and Christopher Norris. *Post-Structuralist Readings of English Poetry.* Cambridge: Cambridge Univ. Press, 1987.

Maclean, Hugh. "Ben Jonson's Poems: Notes on the Ordered Society." In *Essays in English Literature from the Renaissance to the Victorian Age Presented to A. S. P. Woodhouse,* ed. Millar Maclure and F. W. Watt, 43–68. Toronto: Univ. of Toronto Press, 1964.

Manley, Lawrence. *Convention, 1500–1750.* Harvard Univ. Press, 1980. Especially part 4, "Contextualism and the Role of Convention in Historiography," 203–40.

Marcus, Leah Sinanoglou. " 'Present Occasions' and the Shaping of Ben Jonson's Masques." *ELH* 45 (1978): 205–25.

——. "The Occasion of Ben Jonson's *Pleasure Reconciled to Virtue.*" *Studies in English Literature* 19 (1979): 271–93.

——. "Masquing Occasions and Masque Structure." *Research Opportunities in Renaissance Drama* 24 (1981): 7–16.

Markiewicz, Henryk. "Ut Pictura Poesis . . . A History of the Topos and the Problem." *New Literary History* 18 (1987): 535–58.

Marotti, Arthur. "The Self-Reflexive Art of Ben Jonson's *Sejanus.*" *Texas Studies in Literature and Language* 12 (1970): 197–220.

——. "All About Jonson's Poetry." *ELH* 39 (1972): 208–37.

——. "John Donne and the Rewards of Patronage." In *The Patronage in the Renaissance,* ed. Guy Fitch Lytle and Stephen Orgel, 207–34. Princeton: Princeton Univ. Press, 1981.

——. " 'Love Is Not Love': Elizabethan Sonnet Sequences and the Social Order." *ELH* 49 (1982): 396–428.

——. *John Donne, Coterie Poet.* Madison: Univ. of Wisconsin Press, 1986.

Meagher, John C. *Method and Meaning in Jonson's Masques.* Notre Dame, Ind.: Notre Dame Univ. Press, 1966.

Martines, Lauro. *Society and History in English Renaissance Verse.* Oxford: Basil Blackwell, 1985.

Miles, Rosalind. *Ben Jonson: His Life and Work.* London: Routledge and Kegan Paul, 1986.

Montrose, Louis. "Of Gentlemen and Shepherds: The Politics of Elizabethan Pastoral Form." *ELH* 50 (1983): 415–59.

——. "Renaissance Literary Studies and the Subject of History." *English Literary Renaissance* 16 (1986): 5–12.

Murray, Timothy. "From Foul Sheets to Legitimate Model: Antitheater, Text, Ben Jonson." *New Literary History* 14 (1983): 641–64.

Nelson, William. *Fact or Fiction: The Dilemma of the Renaissance Storyteller.* Cambridge: Harvard Univ. Press, 1973.

New Literary History 14, no. 3 (1983). Special issue: *Renaissance Literature and Contemporary Theory.*

Newton, Richard C. " 'Ben./Jonson': The Poet in the Poems." In *Two Renaissance Mythmakers: Christopher Marlowe and Ben Jonson.* Selected Papers from the English Institute, 1975–76. Ed. Alvin Kernan. Baltimore: Johns Hopkins Univ. Press, 1977.

——. "Jonson and the (Re-)Invention of the Book." In *Classic and Cavalier: Essays on Jonson and the Sons of Ben,* ed. Claude J. Summers and Ted-Larry Pebworth, 31–58. Pittsburgh: Univ. of Pittsburgh Press, 1982.

Nichols, John, *The Progresses of James the First.* 4 vols. 1882. Reprint. New York: AMS Press, 1968.

Nicoll, Allardyce. *Stuart Masques and the Renaissance Stage.* 1938. New York: Benjamin Blom, 1963.

Norbrook, David. "The Reformation of the Masque." In *The Court Masque,* 94–110. *See* Lindley.

——. *Poetry and Politics in the English Renaissance.* London: Routledge, 1984.

Norman, Liane. "Risk and Redundancy." *PMLA* 90 (1975): 285–91.

Noyes, Robert Gale. *Ben Jonson on the English Stage, 1660–1776.* Cambridge: Harvard Univ. Press, 1935.

Orgel, Stephen. *The Jonsonian Masque.* Cambridge: Harvard Univ. Press, 1965.

——. *The Illusion of Power: Political Theater in the English Renaissance.* Berkeley and Los Angeles: Univ. of California Press, 1975.

Orgel, Stephen, and Roy Strong. *Inigo Jones: The Theater of the Stuart Court.* Berkeley and Los Angeles: Univ. of California Press, 1973.

Ornstein, Robert. "Ben Jonson." *The Moral Vision of Jacobean Tragedy.* Madison: Univ. of Wisconsin Press, 1960.

Parfit, George A. E. "Virtue and Pessimism in Three Plays by Ben Jonson." *Studies in the Literary Imagination* 6 (1973): 23–40.

Partridge, Edward B. "Ben Jonson's *Epigrammes:* The Named and the Nameless." *Studies in the Literary Imagination* 6 (1972): 153–98.

Patterson, Annabel. *Censorship and Interpretation: The Conditions of Writing and Reading in Early Modern England.* Madison: Univ. of Wisconsin Press, 1984.

Pechter, Edward. "The New Historicism and Its Discontents: Politicizing Renaissance Drama." *PMLA* 102 (1987): 292–303.

Peterson, Richard S. *Imitation and Praise in the Poems of Ben Jonson.* New Haven: Yale Univ. Press, 1981.

Pigman, G. W., III. "Suppressed Grief in Jonson's Funeral Poetry." *English Literary Renaissance* 13 (1983): 203–20.

Plett, Heinrich. "Aesthetic Constituents in the Courtly Culture of Renaissance England." *New Literary History* 14 (1983): 597–621.

Randall, Dale B. J. *Jonson's Gypsies Unmasked: Background and Theme of "The Gypsies Metamorphosed."* Durham, N.C.: Duke Univ. Press, 1975.

Rathmell, J. C. A. "Jonson, Lord Lisle, and Penshurst." *English Literary Renaissance* 1 (1971): 250–60.

Renaissance Drama, n.s. 1. Essays Principally on Masques and Entertainments. Ed. S. Schoenbaum. Evanston, Ill.: Northwestern Univ. Press, 1968.

Righter [Barton], Anne. *Shakespeare and the Idea of Play.* New York: Penguin, 1962.

Rowe, Jr., George E. "Ben Jonson's Quarrel with Audience and Its Renaissance Context." *Studies in Philology* 81 (1984): 438–60.

Sallust. *Conspiracy of Catiline.* Trans. S. A. Handford. New York: Penguin, 1963.

Sharpe, Kevin. *Sir Robert Cotton 1586–1631: History and Politics in Early Modern England.* Oxford: Oxford Univ. Press, 1979.

Shelley, Percy Bysshe. *Charles the First.* In *Poems,* 140–65. Vol. 4 of *The Complete Works.* Ed. Roger Ingpen and Walter E. Peck. The Julian Edition. New York: Charles Scribner's Sons, 1928.

Sidney, Sir Philip. *A Defence of Poetry.* In *Miscellaneous Prose of Sir Philip Sidney,* ed. Katherine Duncan-Jones and Jan Van Dorsten, 59–122. Oxford: Clarendon, 1973.

Simpson, Percy. "Ben Jonson and Cecilia Bulstrode." *TLS,* 6 March 1930, 187.

Sinfield, Alan. "Power and Ideology: An Outline Theory and Sidney's *Arcadia.*" *ELH* 52 (1985): 259–75.

Spingarn, Joel Elias. *A History of Literary Criticism in the Renaissance.* New York: Macmillan, 1899.

Sweeney, John Gordon. *Jonson and the Psychology of Public Theater: To Coin the Spirit, Spread the Soul.* Princeton: Princeton Univ. Press, 1985.

Swinburne, Algernon C. *A Study of Ben Jonson.* London: Chatto & Windus, 1889.

Tacitus. *The Annals of Imperial Rome.* Trans. Michael Grant. London: Cassell, 1963.

Talbert, Ernest William. "The Interpretation of Jonson's Courtly Spectacles." *PMLA* 61 (1949): 454–73.

Trimpi, Wesley. *Ben Jonson's Poems: A Study of the Plain Style.* Stanford, Calif.: Stanford Univ. Press, 1962.

Vickers, Brian. "Epideictic and Epic in the Renaissance." *New Literary History* 14 (1983): 497–538.

Wallerstein, Ruth. *Studies in Seventeenth-Century Poetics.* Madison: Univ. of Wisconsin Press, 1961.

Wayne, Don E. *Penshurst: The Semiotics of Place and the Poetics of History.* Madison: Univ. of Wisconsin Press, 1984.

Wedgwood, C. V. "The Last Masque." In *Truth and Opinion,* 135–56. London: Collins, 1960.

Weimann, Robert. "Past Significance and Present Meaning in Literary History." *New Literary History* 1 (1969): 91–112.

———. *Structure and Society in Literary History: Studies in the History and Theory of Historical Criticism.* Expanded ed. Baltimore: Johns Hopkins Univ. Press, 1984.

Weinberg, Bernard. *A History of Literary Criticism in the Italian Renaissance.* 2 vols. Chicago: Univ. of Chicago Press, 1961.

Weitzman, Francis W. "Notes on the Elizabethan 'Elegie.'" *PMLA* 50 (1935): 435–43.

Welsford, Enid. *The Court Masque.* Cambridge: Cambridge Univ. Press, 1927.

Williams, Raymond. *The Country and the City.* New York: Oxford Univ. Press, 1973.

Wilson, Edmund. "Morose Ben Jonson." In *Ben Jonson: A Collection of Critical Essays,* 60–74. Englewood Cliffs, N.J.: Prentice-Hall, 1963.

Winner, Jack D. "Ben Jonson's *Epigrammes* and the Conventions of Formal Verse Satire." *Studies in English Literature* 23 (1983): 61–76.

Womack, Peter. *Ben Jonson.* Rereading Literature. Ed. Terry Eagleton. Oxford: Basil Blackwell, 1986.

Wright, Louis B. "The Elizabethan Middle-Class Taste for History." *The Journal of Modern History* 3 (1931): 175–97.

Wykes, David. "Ben Jonson's 'Chast Booke'—*The Epigrammes.*" *Renaissance and Modern Studies* 13 (1969): 76–87.

Index